Published by

Periplus Editions (HK) Ltd.

with editorial offices at

153 Milk Street

Boston, MA 02109

and

5 Little Road #08-01

Singapore 536983

Copyright © 2000
Periplus Editions (HK) Ltd.

ALL RIGHTS RESERVED

ISBN: 962-593-534-7

Library of Congress Catalog Number: 99-050251

Credits:

All photography by Jacob Termansen.
Additional photographs by Will van
Overbeek (pages 2, 4, 8–23, 26–28).

Distributors

North America, Latin America, Europe, and the Middle East

Tuttle Publishing

Distrbution Center

Airport Industrial Park

364 Innovation Drive

North Clarendon, VT 05759-9436

Tel: (802) 773-8930

Tel: (800) 526-2778

Japan

Tuttle Publishing

RK Building, 2nd Floor

2-13-10 Shimo-Meguro, Meguro-Ku

Tokyo 153 0064

Tel: (03) 5437-0171

Fax: (03) 5437-0755

Asia-Pacific

Berkeley Books Pte. Ltd.

5 Little Road #08-01

Singapore 536983

Tel: (65) 280-1330

Fax: (65) 280-6290

First Edition

1 3 5 7 9 10 8 6 4 2

06 05 04 03 02 01 00

PRINTED IN SINGAPORE

THE FOOD OF
TEXAS

Authentic Recipes from the Lone Star State

by Caroline Stuart

With additional essays by Dotty Griffith

Featuring recipes from the following Texas restaurants:

Reata Restaurant
Star Canyon
Laurels
Cafe Annie
Américas
The Mansion on Turtle Creek

DeVille Restaurant
Ruggles Grill
Boulevard Bistrot
Las Canarias
Pappas Brothers Steakhouse

Photography by Jacob Termansen and Will van Overbeek
Styling by Christina Ong

PERIPLUS

Contents

Part One: Food in Texas

From the prairies to the Gulf Coast, the Lone Star State has it all

by Caroline Stuart

When we think of Texas, it is inevitable—and expected—that legend springs to mind. It is, after all, the second-largest state in the U.S. and home to larger-than-life legends Buddy Holly, Lyndon B. Johnson, Scott Joplin, and Gene Autry. From its panhandle on down to the Gulf of Mexico and the Rio Grande, Texas is filled to its ten-gallon brim with cattle drives and chuck wagon meals, ornery longhorn steer, and oil gushers spewing black gold.

Everything here is *big*, from its prairies, to its ranches, to its oil baron mansions. Make no mistake, the Lone Star State is known for the serious appetites of its loyal Texans. And the history of Texas food is equally impressive. Over hundreds of years, its culinary heart and soul has been shaped by countless inhabitants, each stirring their own ingredients into timeless Lone Star recipes.

Just sample this diversity for yourself. Early Spanish explorers found Native Americans making fry bread, raising vegetables, and flavoring their food with local pecans. Chicken-fried steak, a Texas classic, was an adaptation of German immigrants' beloved Wiener schnitzel. And in San Antonio, Mexican buñuelos are still a Christmas tradition. Each region has a style of food to boast about, resulting in fascinating cross-cultural creations. In fact, it's not unusual for a pot of fiery chili to share a table with crunchy Southern fried chicken, German bacon-laced potato salad, and Mexican nachos. All to be washed down with margaritas or ice-cold beer.

The state's location provides the backdrop for this rich, varied cuisine. The Gulf Coast supports a thriving seafood industry; Texas wineries have existed since 1662 when Franciscan priests discovered local grapes. Strong culinary influences from neighboring Mexico permeate menus throughout the state. Long ties to the colonial South put peach cobbler on the tables of East Texas, while Cajun cooks from Louisiana introduced gumbos. Other immigrant influences arrived from farther afield, providing more intrigue to the mix: Spanish chorizo sausage and fruit-filled Czech pastries.

Eating establishments vary as much as the fare. Barbecue joints remain justly famous for succulent brisket, ribs, and chicken. Urban cowboys crowd upscale restaurants to savor farm-raised ostrich and foie gras. At steak houses, beef connoisseurs sip martinis and devour steaks that may weigh a full pound. Simply put, Texans in boots and jeans or sequins and silk are making the most of the most, whether their meal came from a Texas cattle ranch or a traditional Mexican kitchen. Legend aside, a Texan's kitchen is ground zero for a meal you won't soon forget. Yahoo!

Opposite:
Patron John Boutin prepares to devour a crispy-fried tower of onion rings at Restaurant Biga in San Antonio. He'll wash it down with a bottle of Shiner Bock beer, brewed locally in Shiner, Texas.

Culinary History of Texas

From ranch house to wursthaus,
the influences on Texas cuisine might surprise you

by Dotty Griffith

The chuck wagon was the country's first take-out restaurant. Drawn by horse or mule, it would follow the roundup twice yearly to the outermost reaches of the ranch and provide food, utensils, bedrolls, and medical supplies to cowboys. The "Cookie" would prepare food for the evening, the cowboys would help in the clean-up, and entertainment by harmonica would precede the night's hard-earned slumber.

In Texas, as in other areas throughout the United States and the world, multiple influences—historic, ethnic, geographic, and climatic—converge to shape the local cuisine. But few places can claim the diversity of Texas. In turn, Texas cooking traditions, along with those of neighboring regions, have been transformed by contemporary chefs into the robust and innovative modern culinary movement known as Southwestern cuisine.

In the fifteenth and sixteenth centuries, Spaniards arrived in the colonies that would become Mexico and Texas. Not only did they bring European culinary traditions, they also brought Central American chiles. It was to be the beginning of a long and delicious relationship which spanned 300 years and left its mark firmly on the cuisine. Flavors, techniques, and ingredients from south of the border remain evident in Texas today. And though Texas broke from Mexico in 1836, Texicans (as early Texans were known) never forsook the culinary staples of tortillas, refried beans, and enchiladas.

In the early nineteenth century, many settlers came from the Deep South, introducing Texans to culinary traditions from states such as Louisiana and Arkansas. Consequently, the food ways of Southerners, including the defining culinary influence of African slaves, left a lasting impression on Texans' tables. Likewise, a strong French heritage—Cajun and Creole dishes arrived from the Texas-Louisiana border and the upper Gulf Coast—is also deliciously significant. From fried chicken to black-eyed peas to Cajun shrimp, many Texans' favorite dishes whistle Dixie.

Gastronomic impact also came from more unlikely sources. Throughout the 1800s, boatloads of German immigrants, fleeing political upheaval, disembarked along the Gulf Coast, particularly in Galveston, and made Texas their home. Many then made their way to the heart of the state, known today as the Hill Country. The influence of the Germans' skill at smoking meat and concocting pungent sausages is apparent in the classic Texas barbecue. And it's no coincidence that a chicken-fried steak—a staple of truck stops and country cookin' chain restaurants—looks a lot like a Wiener schnitzel.

Although seldom recognized for their cuisine, Native Americans—again, mainly through immigration—played important early roles in the state's food history and production. Texas is best known as a territory that was populated by Plains tribes such as buffalo-hunting Comanches, Apaches, and Kiowas. In fact, it has been home to more tribes than any other state. Vast land areas made Texas a logical deportation destination for displaced members of the Choctaws, Chicka-saws, Cherokees, Creeks, and Semi-noles. Uprooted from their homes in the southeastern United States, they were driven to Texas, where they continued their relatively sophisti-cated ways with food.

Many tribes were so advanced, culinarily speaking, they could prepare corn forty ways. And members of the Caddos tribe, native to East Texas, were accomplished farmers who raised corn, beans, and squash. Sixteenth-century Spanish missionaries who settled in the area were impressed by the display of cooking skills they witnessed. They described an early form of the tamale in their writ-ings, a sort of cornmeal dumpling wrapped in a corn husk or banana leaf and steamed. Although we

The Texas citrus industry was established in the early 1880s when Don Macedonio Vela planted seedling orange trees at the Laguna Seca Ranch in the Lower Rio Grande Valley. Grapefruit orchards were established in Texas in the 1920s–30s, and the success of these led to the state's reputation as a high-quality red grapefruit producer.

think of tamales as having Spanish roots, they are more likely of Native American origin.

The varied geography and climate of Texas, a state somewhat larger than the country of France, also accounts for a vast array of ingredients, flavor, and techniques. Windy grasslands of the Panhan-dle suffer extremes of hot and cold. Desert moun-tains and ranges of West Texas and the Hill Country bask in hot days and cool nights. The fertile valley of South Texas, the coastal plains, and the Gulf Coast enjoy year-round mild temperatures. The farmlands of central and northeast Texas cycle through hot summers and wet, cold winters. And the piney woods and bayous of East Texas swelter in the same heat and humidity that dampens neighboring Louisiana. It's little wonder that the state yields such a variety of foods.

After World War II, Texan cuisine was also spiced up with variety. Up to and during the war, Texas had enjoyed an interesting, although unsophisticated, style of cooking that varied from area to area, but which enjoyed only scant influence from outside. During the war, however, soldiers from all over the United States brought their tastes to Texas, which had become a major military training ground. More importantly, postwar Texas GIs returned from overseas having sampled foods they had never eaten at home. There were hints of change on the culinary horizon for Texans.

At the Kim Son Restaurant in Austin, Diem Nguyen (co-owner Kim Tran's niece) holds up the specialty of the house: bo nuong xa *or grilled beef roll.*

The postwar economy transformed Texas from a rural and largely agricultural state into an economic power driven by oil, finance, industry, and technology. Social changes and an increasingly mobile population created more curious and demanding consumers. Even though a few outposts of culinary civilization existed, such as the Old Warsaw in Dallas, the chili parlors, coffee shops, mom-and-pop cafes, and barbecue shacks remained the predominant eating emporiums.

The real change in Texas dining occurred via a source seldom credited with cultural advancement: the state legislature. In 1971, on-premise consumption of alcoholic beverages was legalized. Until that time, beer, wine, or any other alcoholic beverage couldn't be sold and consumed in the same spot—the reality was that customers brown-bagged liquor into even the finest restaurants. At about the same time, food awareness and culinary chic began in earnest on the East and West Coasts, fed by the popularity of television cooking shows and the growing interest in fine wining and dining.

In Europe, they had nouvelle cuisine; in the United States, it was New American. Regional cuisines—developed by young chefs interested in adapting fresh, indigenous ingredients and traditional recipes into haute cuisine—flourished in a national atmosphere of experimentation, curiosity, and demand for innovation.

The change in state alcoholic beverage laws came at just the right time for Texas to participate in the national awakening to regional cuisines. Houston and Dallas were the primary centers for the birth of a culinary style that would come to be known as Southwestern cuisine. Robert Del Grande brought his uniquely scientific style to Cafe Annie in Houston, creating wonderfully cohesive dishes from varying ingredients. Stephan Pyles, then of Routh Street Cafe, began creating fancy dishes out of simple food and was praised by *Bon Appétit* for "almost single-handedly changing the cooking scene in Texas." And Dean Fearing, of The Mansion on Turtle Creek, caused quite a stir with his innovative and stylish lobster taco: lobster meat rolled in a flour tortilla and served with mango salsa. Despite some conservative critique, consumers loved it and it's now one of his signature dishes.

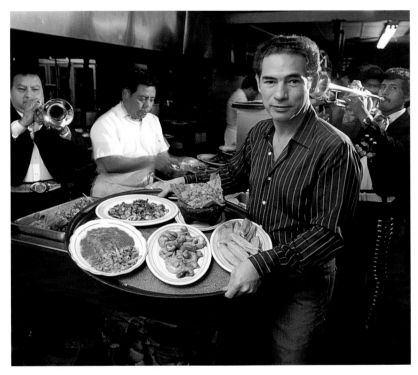

Mario Cantu of Mario's Mexican Restarant serves up authentic Tex-Mex while a mariachi band accompanies.

All this sophistication hasn't dimmed Texans' love for the food of childhood. During spring and fall, barbecue and chili cook-offs abound throughout the state. Rival organizations devoted to the preparation of the perfect bowl of red, and to the consumption of large quantities of beer, hold world championship cook-offs each year in Terlingua, a remote, almost ghostly town in the Davis Mountains of far West Texas. Across the state, Czechs hold an annual festival in the town of West (between Dallas and Austin) to celebrate their favorite pastry, the *kolache*. San Antonio and Austin still have some of the best Mexican food in the state. And along the Gulf Coast, neighbors gather on a weekend afternoon for crab and crawfish boils.

The food of Texas ranges from homestyle fare to more sophisticated preparations turned out by some of the most refined restaurant kitchens in the country. Many Texans are proud to say they appreciate both of these culinary extremes for their unique character and flavor. That's a heritage worth preserving.

The Biggest and the Best of Texas

Fact, fantasy, and wishful thinking

by Caroline Stuart

It's hard for Texans to be humble. Their bumper stickers proclaim "I wasn't born in Texas but I got here as soon as I could" and "Don't mess with Texas," suggesting that Texas is not only a state, but a state of mind. Typical residents brag that their state has the biggest and best of nearly everything, from the most stars in the sky to the world's biggest moon. They might even lay claim to living in "God's country" and declare that you have to go through Texas to get to Heaven. Doubters, they might tell you, are cordially invited to stick around and see for themselves.

While such bravado might seem shameless to the uninitiated, Texans needn't look far to find facts to support their pride. For openers, the Lone Star State is eight hundred miles wide with incredibly vast stretches of land and open sky, but that's only the beginning. Among its many ranches, Texas boasts the largest in the country. In fact, the King Ranch spreads across more than 800,000 acres. That's more acreage than the state of Rhode Island!

In 1853, riverboat captain Richard King bought this South Texas spread for only three dollars an acre for 15,500 acres of land. Then he stocked it with longhorn cattle, at five dollars per head. Today, vast herds of cattle roam the ranges of King Ranch, known as the birthplace of the American ranching industry. And since its inception a century and a half ago, it has founded two American beef brands and produced some of the all-time top running and performance horses.

For the curious-minded who aren't steeped in the traditions of life on the range, Texas also has more dude ranches than any other state. Here, city slickers and cowboy wanna-bes can get a taste of ranch life. After a day in the saddle, a trailside cookout of sizzling Texas-sized steaks, baked beans, home fries, and pecan pie makes a home on the range pretty appealing—and might provide the casual visitor with some insight into the nature of Texan cuisine.

Whether on the range or in city restaurants—and no matter what the dish—plates come to the

Opposite:
The legendary 1.2 million-acre King Ranch lies twenty miles south of Corpus Christi, and was established in the 1850s by Richard King. Pictured here are Darwin Smith (foreground) and Tio Kleburg (background).

This page:
At the annual Chili Cook-off, held near San Marcos, chili aficionados throw their hat into the ring to compete against other contestants' concoctions. Some participants guard generations-old secret recipes, while other participants' ingredients are, well, not so secret.

black-eyed peas are all grown here. And Texas sweet onions—similar to Vidalia, Maui, and Walla Walla onions—are quite famous. Some folks (especially Texans) swear that they are the biggest, sweetest, juiciest onions in the world—and mild enough to eat raw like apples.

And speaking of sweet and juicy, some of the finest citrus in the country thrives in the ideal climate of the Rio Grande Valley, including the Texas state fruit, the Rio Red grapefruit. Rice is another important Texas crop. Exotic strains like Texmati, pecan-scented, and jasmine share the soil with the more familiar long-grain white.

If Texas valleys and farmlands contribute some of the best produce and beef to Texan cuisine, then Southeast Texas coaxes another ingredient from the Gulf of Mexico. Everyday, shrimpers bring in huge hauls of America's favorite seafood to be fried, boiled, sautéed, souped, and sauced. Local shrimp are prized throughout the state and shipped nation-wide. To fulfill the constant demand, commercial shrimp farming supplements the supply from the Gulf.

table piled high with huge portions. But beef is the preferred fare, and no wonder: Texas is the country's leading cattle-raising state, contributing a major share to the local economy. And select cuts of the stuff, served on its own or in a hearty chili, can be had in the state's many popular steak houses.

Texas is by no means strictly carnivorous however. Its farms provide an enormous supply of produce, including much of the nation's winter crop. Wheat, spinach, watermelon, cantaloupes, straw-berries, pecans, chiles, peaches, potatoes, and

With such a variety of foods native to the region, Texans love to celebrate the heritage that has contributed to their cuisine, and they pull out all the stops to do so. From one end of the state to the other, good folks gather the best from their crop, game, and cattle to honor an area's specialties. On the fruity side, you can partake in the Poteet Strawberry Festival, Fredericksburg Peach Festival, and Pecos Cantaloupe Festival. And the Luling Watermelon

Thump is punctuated by a seed-spitting competition that the locals take quite seriously.

For those who prefer stick-to-your-ribs samplings, there's the Wurstfest in New Braunfels, with a decidedly German flair; the East Texas Poultry Festival in the town of Center, with a lively flying-chicken contest; the Black-Eyed Pea Festival in Athens; the World Champion Barbecue Goat Cook-Off in Brady; and the Official Shrimporee of Texas in Aransas Pass. And for the strong of tongue and heart, the Palestine Hot Pepper Festival, the "hottest festival in Texas," features a chile-eating contest. Attendees might tell you that, short of a blowtorch, there's nothing too hot for a bold Texan to put in his mouth, and here the chile reigns supreme. But the celebrations don't end there. Barbecue festivals turn up all over, and everyone awaits the results of the granddaddy of chili cook-offs in Terlingua.

But this famous down-home character is counterbalanced by the state's equally famous opulent glamour and conspicuous consumption. For every pair of broken-in cowboy boots dancing the two-step and making tracks to local barbecues and cafes, a stylish couple dressed in glitter and gold savors haute cuisine in Houston, Austin, or Dallas. Whether in a low-down honky-tonk down the road from the farm or at a refined upscale establishment in a big city, it's impossible to miss the genuine hospitality, warm southern drawl, and easy comfortable attitude that emanates.

In light of this fabulous diversity of cuisine and culture, one fact remains: the Texas soil, forever

At La Fogata Restaurant in San Antonio, owner Johnny Cavillo helps his friend Marla eat queso flameado, prepared with Mexican sausage, cheese from Oaxaca, and corn or flour tortillas.

yielding and forever stretching to where it meets the sky, provides.

So if Texans speak of their fair state in bold superlatives, perhaps the bragging rights are justified, even if exaggeration does creep in from time to time. Who can blame Texans for taking pride in what is truly one of the most colorful of the United States, for celebrating their shindigs and state fairs, shining cities and sprawling plains, the best beef and barbecue in the world, and on and on. The state is surely blessed with bounty.

The Mexican Connection

The exciting fusion of Tex-Mex takes Texas by storm
by Dotty Griffith

Although Texas freed itself from Mexico in 1836, Texans were never so foolish as to seek culinary independence. On the contrary, they've embraced the spicy flavors, colorful ingredients, and traditional techniques from south of the border and made them their own.

Tex-Mex cuisine grew out of the combined cultures of Texas and Mexico. Most of the dishes are simple fare, usually combining beans, corn, and a bit of meat. Tex-Mex icons include tacos, tamales, burritos, fajitas, enchiladas, refried beans, nachos, and Mexican or "red" rice, so-called because it is cooked with tomatoes. Variations on these dishes have spread all over the United States—arguably the world—in the form of fast food, although what is served in New York or Seattle seldom bears resemblance to the real thing.

Mexican cuisine (also known as "Mex-Mex") is dynamic enough by itself. Its source is in simple, no-frills food from a vast number of climates (deserts, mountains, rainforests, and temperate coastlines, for example), and it honors the traditions of Native Americans and Europeans, primarily Spanish. But it ranks as one of the world's most complex and varied cuisines, especially if one bases such assessments on the variety and refinement of sauces. With hundreds of salsas and moles, Mexican cuisine can strike as many chords as French or Chinese. Just imagine what it can accomplish when it's teamed up with Texan cuisine.

Tex-Mex flair isn't necessarily the same in all parts of the state. Indeed, aficionados will argue that the cuisine differs distinctly from city to city.

San Antonio is the most Mexican of all the Texas cities, and the food reflects that. This is where chili con carne (a bowl of red) was first sold from street carts by women known as chili queens. The carts were an antecedent to the chili parlors that were once as common in some Texas towns as Dairy Queens are today. San Antonio boasts restaurants like La Fogata—"The Torch"—where legendary *New York Times* writer Craig Claiborne "discovered"

Opposite:
Mama Ninfa Laurenzo herself serves up some of the best Tex-Mex the state has to offer at her self-titled establishment, Ninfa's, located in Houston.
This page:
You'll find the strongest Mexican connection among Texas residents in San Antonio, where holidays such as Cinco de Mayo and Diecisés de Septiembre are celebrated much as they would be in Mexico. Here, young folk dancers participate in the revelry at the Mission San Jose y San Miguel de Aguaya in San Antonio during a Mariachi Mass.

queso flameado (flaming cheese), an appetizer of melted white Mexican cheese flamed with brandy. Locals swear by El Mirador, with its distinctive fruit tacos and grilled goat. And no matter where you go in San Antonio, a party isn't a party without *anticuchos* (grilled marinated beef or chicken chunks on a skewer).

Tex-Mex in Dallas was originally pretty simple: enchiladas or tamales with what Texans call chile gravy, rice, beans, and, almost exclusively, corn tortillas, plus a praline for dessert. This uncomplicated tradition spawned the two restaurant chains that for decades defined Tex-Mex cuisine: El Fenix and El Chico. Among small local operations, Martin's Cocina and Rafa's stand out, as does Mia's for fajitas. Gloria's offers an enchanting combination of Savadoran and Mexican cuisines.

Joe T. Garcia's in Fort Worth, perhaps the best known Mexican restaurant in Texas, also remains true to its simple roots. Family owned, this rambling restaurant has lots of outdoor seating and covers almost a whole city block.

Over in Austin, a bold restaurateur has dared to innovate. Matt Martinez' El Rancho Martinez has fed generations of University of Texas students cheaply but well. Now with three additional Dallas restaurants under his belt, Matt takes some of his

The Las Manitas ("Little Hands") Avenue Cafe in Austin is an authentic Mexican eatery owned by the Perez sisters: Cynthia (middle) and Lidia (right). On the left is Elsa Lemus, one of the cooks at Las Manitas'.

tried-and-true fare and dares to improve it. One great example: the recombinant Bob Armstrong dip—a layered appetizer of guacamole, refried beans, and *chile con queso* (melted cheese dip)—which is named after the former Texas land commissioner for whom it was created. Also in Austin, consider Guero's, Las Manitas, and Angie's. The latter offers freshly made corn tortillas that you'll never forget. And for a fully authentic experience, Fonda San Miguel is a tribute to true Mexican cuisine.

Ninfa Laurenzo of Houston built a restaurant dynasty on the addictive properties of her warm guacamole salsa. Ninfa's remains one of the city's—and state's—best, retaining the integrity and flavor that made Mama Ninfa famous. Also in Houtson, Blue Agave serves a good upscale Southwestern meal.

El Paso in the far western part of the state offers Mexican food like nowhere else, although it seems more akin to that of neighboring New Mexico than the rest of Texas, but without the blue corn. Roasted green chiles are the backbone of its daring cuisine, providing the distinguishing characteristic of its uniquely delicious Mexican food. The well-known La Hacienda is now even more remarkable for its setting than for its food, set on four acres and adorned with artwork and historical monuments. And the oddly named, but much loved, H and H Car Wash and Coffee Shop is an El Paso institution where everyone loves to "eat Mexican" in the small dive next to the car wash.

No discussion of the influence of Mexican culture and cuisine in Texas is worth having without paying tribute to some individual Tex-Mex specialties. The Mexican breakfast *menudo*, a tripe stew, is purported to cure even the worst hangover. While not for culinary cowards, other traditional dishes like *migas* (eggs scrambled with onions, peppers, tomatoes, and strips of day-old corn tortillas), or *huevos rancheros* (fried eggs on a corn tortilla smothered in salsa roja) are some of the easiest dishes of the Tex-Mex breakfast repertoire to embrace, especially when served with a side of silken refried beans, made smooth, glossy and incomparable with lard.

Fajitas have enjoyed a rise in national popularity. For years a traditional favorite on South Texas ranches where they originated, it wasn't until the 1980s that a nationwide fascination with regional dishes and Mesquite grilling combined to spread the word all over the state and eventually the rest of the country. A Dallas chain, On the Border, has preached the fajita gospel well beyond the Red River, into 27 states and as far north as Michigan.

Texas also gets credit for several modern Tex-Mex innovations. Whether you love 'em or

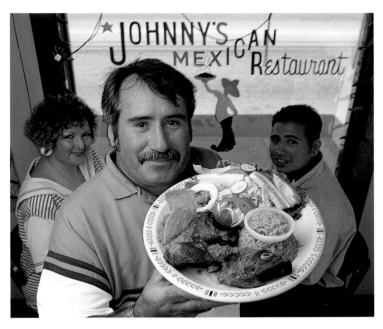

Johnny's Mexican Restaurant in San Antonio is famous for its cabrito—*a delicacy of tender young goat meat traditionally prepared in an earth pit oven.*

loathe 'em, ballpark nachos (melted processed cheese poured over tortilla chips with optional pickled jalapeño slices) originated at the Texas Rangers home field in Arlington and are now served all over the country. And the popularity of fruit slush drinks catapulted the classic Mexican cocktail, the margarita, into the frozen drink limelight.

Frankly, it's utterly impossible not to find good Tex-Mex just about anywhere in Texas, although the closer you get to the border, the more likely it is you'll find something authentic and fresh. If you can't find it, just ask around. Every Texan claims to be an authority on where to get the best. At least you know you'll be getting one expert's opinion.

Where's the Beef?

Chili, butt rubs, and big buns
by Caroline Stuart

Where's the beef? Texas has it! Beef and the backyard grill are practically sacred in the state, and a barbecue is the cornerstone for countless social gatherings. Politicians use barbecues as platforms for delivering campaign promises, and hosts of family reunions use them to ensure a good time had by all. Larger-than-life, cattle-baron-style events are still held, too, and any or no excuse at all will guarantee a crowd, whether the occasion is a church supper or the Fourth of July. But barbecues are not limited to large functions; it's practically mandatory for a Texan to be able to cook outside at home, and most Texans seem to have an insatiable craving to do just that. The many warm months make it possible to move the kitchen to the patio.

The word *barbecue* is commonly used to refer to the simple process of cooking outdoors. But the methods vary wildly, depending on whether the food is over a charcoal or a wood fire or on a gas grill. Grilling food over a hot wood fire is the oldest method of cooking. Nowadays, the wood fire takes the form of prepared charcoal chunks, or briquets. Grilling is a fast and effective way to cook, but little additional flavor is obtained, especially for quick cooking items. Smoking—that is, cooking in a pit barbecue or wood smoker—uses the heat and smoke of hardwood chips to cook meats slowly, gradually infusing them with the smoky taste real barbecue lovers demand.

Every self-respecting outdoor cook has his or her own favorite method, temperature, times, rubs, sauces, woods, and specialties, the merits of which are often hotly debated. After the smoking process, some folks season their meat with a rub, a mixture of dried herbs and spices that is massaged into the meat before it is cooked, producing a wonderfully flavorful crust. Rub recipes are limited only by your imagination; sauces and mops are much the same. There are as many secret recipes for sauces as there are folks doing the barbecuing, but among the folks who prefer to add sauce, the tomato-based varieites predominate. Nearly everyone, however, agrees on the requisite

Opposite:
New tires and delicious barbecue, sold in one place. The slow-smoked beef brisket is a specialty.
This page:
The Mikeska brothers—or Barbecue Brothers, as they have come to be known—are meat-on-the-grill connoisseurs. Each of them owns their own barbecue restaurant, in six different areas of the state.

Opposite:
*Barbecue pork
ribs are the
specialty of the
day at the Mt.
Zion Missionary
Baptist Church
Barbecue in
Huntsville.*
*This Page:
City Market
Barbecue, located
in Schulenburg, is
famous for its
jalapeño sausage,
and is credited
with its invention.*

Fletcher Davis introduced it at the St. Louis World's Fair in 1904. Regardless, Texans love their hamburgers, and burgers served in Texas can pack in as much as twelve ounces of ground beef. The ideal hamburger is grilled crisp on the outside and juicy on the inside. Piled high with layers of cheese, lettuce, tomato, onion, and pickle, and anointed with mustard or mayonnaise, it makes a good meal with a casual Texas attitude.

Beef has a long history in Texas. In 1893, Amarillo's population was "between 500 and 600 people and 50,000 head of cattle." It is used in countless dishes. Indeed, some surveys tell us that hundreds of thousands of the popular specialty known as chicken-fried steak (battered and fried steak) are eaten every day in Texas. Tex-Mex food showcases beef in beef-filled *tacos al carbon*, and in El Paso the signature dish is shredded brisket *salpicón* salad.

accompaniments. Simply put, no barbecue would be complete without baked beans, coleslaw, and corn bread or that thickly sliced, crispy Texas toast. But a slice of white loaf bread will do just fine.

Year-round, you'll find good old-fashioned fun at Texas barbecue festivals or cook-offs. Just look for smoke, and follow your nose to the pits and pit meisters who start tending their smokers before daybreak. Soon, you'll join other barbecue fanatics, hundreds or even thousands, who travel great distances for the lip-smacking taste of long-cooked ribs, mopped chicken, highly seasoned sausage, and the pièce de résistance, dry-rubbed brisket of beef.

Beef at its most basic—the hamburger—has had a secure spot in the hearts of Americans for years. Several states have claimed its invention, but Texas insists that it originated here in the 1880s, and Texan

The Lone Star State works its charm on visitors, many of whom regularly succumb to buying a pair of cowboy boots and tucking into a big steak dinner or rack of ribs before crossing back over the border. Competition among barbecue joints is fierce—you can't drive far in the state without passing one. They're usually modest places where you eat from paper or plastic plates and sit at wooden picnic tables in the shade. But beef and barbecue are subjects passionate enough to make hearts flutter. So who knows, maybe those visitors won't leave Texas after all. Many don't.

Around the State

Creative chefs are redefining Texas cuisine
by Dotty Griffith

Texas chefs are a wild bunch. Many wear cowboy boots in the kitchen. Some strum guitars when they're not working. But all take dead aim at preparing food that is as imaginative and as distinctive as they are. Texas first showed up on the nation's culinary radar screen in the 1980s, when Dean Fearing, Stephan Pyles, and Robert Del Grande spearheaded the Southwestern cuisine movement. Their paths have since diverged in recent years. Dean Fearing, with several books and a television series to his credit, continues as executive chef of Rosewood Hotels and The Mansion on Turtle Creek in Dallas. His signature Southwestern cuisine is sublime.

A waitress at the Granite Café in Austin clears out of the proverbial kitchen when a pretend quarrel between chefs heats up.

Stephan Pyles detoured from the "new Texas cuisine" road when he opened Dallas' "global seafood" restaurant, AquaKnox. Later he joined forces with Carlson Restaurants Worldwide (parent company of T.G.I. Friday's), which put him on the trail of expansion, soon opening Star Canyon in Dallas.

Now he's part of the chef stampede to Las Vegas, where he has opened a second Star Canyon. Also busy with books and television, Pyles is developing a casual, relatively inexpensive Mexican taco bar concept, called Canonita.

Houston's Robert Del Grande, known for taking cowboy cuisine upscale, continues as the creative force behind the award-winning Cafe Annie. He also created an easygoing taco bar, Taco Milagro, and Rio Ranch Texas at the Hilton Westchase Hotel.

While these three chefs continue to be the state's best-known restaurant personalities, a whole new talented crew is on the rise. And although Houston and Dallas, the state's largest cities, continue to dominate the culinary scene, Austin, Fort Worth, San Antonio, and El Paso are turning out first-rate restaurants and chefs of note and acclaim.

In recent years, Dallas-Fort Worth has become the third largest market for prime beef, behind New York and Chicago. That means steak houses are nearly as common as cowboy boots on the local streets. Places like Del Frisco's, Al Biernat's, Bob's Steak and Chophouse, Chamberlains, The (Dallas) Palm, and Pappas Bros. Steakhouse (in both Dallas and Houston) are always at the top of the list whenever someone asks for a good spot to tuck into a big porterhouse.

Of course, beef is not all there is to Dallas dining. Danielle Custer of Laurels the Westin Park Central Hotel, and Doug Brown of Nana Grill, at the Wyndham Anatole, are two of the city's best young chefs. Custer was even recently named a *Food and Wine* magazine Rising Star. Their global reach for ingredients, techniques, and daring combinations—including African, Asian, and American flavors—makes their food a wonderful adventure that is garnering national attention.

Chef Kent Rathbun, a disciple of Dean Fearing, was the chef to watch during his stints at the Landmark Restaurant and at Seventeen Seventeen. He went on hiatus for a brief period but has returned as strong as ever with the opening of Abacus, a stunning setting in which he serves equally stunning Asian fusion cuisine to crowds of happy Dallas diners. And elsewhere in Dallas, Tom Fleming is bringing the luster back to the Riviera, which in the past was considered one of the great temples of local French cuisine. Chef Chris Ward is doing double duty, making waves at both The Mercury and Citizen. At the former he serves plates that marry

Who concocted the original margarita? It's reportedly named after the woman who invented it—and Margarita Sames (pictured left) will tell you she's the one. Will that be frozen, or on the rocks?

New American food with Mediterranean cuisine, while his more recent venture, Citizen, is a Euro-Asian combination restaurant and sushi bar. But when folks are hungry for good, old Mex-Mex food, that is, classic Mexican dishes, they head for Javier's or La Valentina.

Just thirty miles west of Dallas, in Fort Worth, Grady Spears of Reata serves cowboy cuisine that charms and satisfies. In addition to his *Cowboy in*

the Kitchen cookbook, he has *Cowboy Cocktails* on the way, plus he has opened a second Reata on oh-so-glitzy Rodeo Drive in Beverly Hills. Back in Fort Worth, Louise Lamensdorf pleases diners at her Bistro Louise, with its suave Mediterranean menu, and Michael Thomson continues to serves up contemporary ranch cuisine at his eponymous Michael's.

Houston's restaurant scene is one of the most vibrant in the state. Michael Cordua, of Houston's Churrascos and Americas, was one of the first chefs in the country to look beyond Mexican cuisine to the tables of South America. A native of Nicaragua, Cordua gambled that Texans were ready for dishes like *churrasco,* beef tenderloin with a piquant *chimichurri* sauce. So far, he's winning.

Other chefs have been busy developing new ideas as well. The latest ventures of veteran Bruce Molzan, of the popular Ruggles Grill and the Galleria-based Grille 5115, is Bistro Latino, specializing in Latino cuisine and live music, as well as the Ruggles Café Bakery. As if that were not enough, Molzan plans to build the only independently owned restaurant in Houston's new downtown Ballpark at Union Station.

Tim Keating at DeVille, in the Four Seasons Hotel, sustains a high level of culinary creativity. His fundamentally French cuisine speaks with an American regional accent. Chef-owner Monica Pope also has a French connection. Her Boulevard Bistrot is about the closest thing you'll find to a French sidewalk cafe in Houston. Despite the carefully crafted European atmosphere, Pope's sometimes daring plates are a celebration of the New American kitchen.

Among the old-time venues in Houston is the well-known Tony's, serving Continental and Italian cuisines, as well as Rotisserie for Beef and Bird, which boasts a top-flight wine list. Chef Mark Cox, who spent time behind the stove at Tony's, is now earning recognition with his own place, Mark's American Cuisine.

Austin is home to the state's most enthusiastic food community, a crowd of diehard boosters who avidly embrace Lone Star wines and products. No chefs exemplify the Austin—and Texas—spirit more than Hudson's on the Bend chef-owner Jeff Blank and executive chef Jay Moore, who are known for their ways with wild game and other regional favorites. Their toques are literally afire on the cover of their new book, *Cooking Fearlessly: Stories and Adventures.* Austin is also the place to find David Garrido's

Opposite: Reata Restaurant in Fort Worth before the lunch rush.
This page: *San Antonio's Riverwalk is lined with outdoor cafes and attracts visitors from around the world.*

Opposite:
Chef Miguel Ravago is the founder of Fonda San Miguel, a well-known authentic Mexican restaurant in Austin. One of the Southwest's top chefs, Ravago is co-author of the award-winning cookbook Concina de la Familia *and is a James Beard Award recipient.*

This page:
Founded in 1976, the Llano Estacado Vineyards is the first modern winery of Texas. Winner of national and international awards, the Llano Estacado has emerged as the state's fastest growing winery.

San Antonio stretches along the river of the same name. Here, New Jersey native Scott Cohen, chef at La Mansion del Rio Hotel, has taken well to Texas ingredients. His natural culinary curiosity inspired a quick study of indigenous herbs and everyday favorites like tacos and enchiladas, which he has recast in a new, upmarket style. His dinnertime crowds prove that San Antonio's citizens like what he is doing. Meanwhile, award-winning chef Bruce Auden, known for his Restaurant BIGA, opened Biga on the Banks in early 2000. Located on the riverside, it offers New American cuisine with a Mediterranean flair.

Because it is tucked down in the far southwestern corner of the state, El Paso sometimes seems closer in spirit to New Mexico than Texas, but it is actually a culinary world unto itself. Yet chef-owner Trae Apodaca's Cafe Central, with its expertly realized contemporary regional flavors, is a match for any restaurant in the state. Across the street, The Dome, in the Camino Real Hotel, is yet another treasure that calls this community on the Rio Grande home.

Jeffrey's, one of city's most popular destinations. Garrido, a Stephan Pyles's protégé, has also co-authored a lively cookbook called *Nuevo Tex-Mex,* which delivers dozens of recipes featuring his distinctive take on contemporary Texas cuisine. If you are a traditionalist, you might head instead for Fonda San Miguel, where the kitchen is renowned for its classic Mexican cuisine.

Chefs in Texas are growing in number and sophistication. While the state remains proud of its Tex-Mex and barbecue traditions, the men and women behind its restaurant stoves are creating an up-to-the-minute culinary reputation built on adventurous flavors, experience, and, most of all, expertise. In other words, this wild bunch is serving great food to appreciative Texans from one end of the state to the other.

Part Two: The Texas Kitchen

Grills, smokers, or pits are essential items
for the serious Texan chef

The equipment in a Texas kitchen does not differ much from that found in any kitchen. In addition to such household items as sharp knives and pots and pans, a heavy cast-iron skillet is perfect for baking corn bread and cooking crisp fried chicken. And while it is nice to have a deep fryer, a heavy saucepan will suffice.

A blender is handy for puréeing sauces and soups and for making frozen drinks like margaritas. For spices, you'll get a lot of use from an electric spice mill, or you can use a mortar and pestle if you want to crush them by hand. Other gadgets, such as a cheese grater and a juicer or reamer for fruit, will make a recipe go together more easily.

Since cooking outdoors is serious business in Texas, some sort of outside cooker is almost mandatory. It can be a simple gas, electric, or charcoal grill or, of course, if money is no object, an elaborate one. If you have a smoker, too, you're equipped to cook up anything under the sun. Failing all of these, a broiler can be substituted for a grill in most cases.

If you decide to shop for a smoker, vertical water smokers are easy to use and inexpensive. The fire is in the bottom, with a couple of cooking racks above it. A water pan rests in between to add the necessary moisture. On the other hand, if you don't want to tend the fire and regulate the heat, buy an electric smoker and throw in some wood chips for flavor. For those who are truly passionate about smoking, consider a pit. A pit is a long cooker that operates as an indirect smoker, with a drum, called a "firebox," attached to one end. The drum holds the fire, and the smoke is channeled from there into the cooking chamber, where you put the meat. Wood chips or chunks are a necessity for flavoring food cooked outdoors. Among the choices that work well are mesquite, hickory, pecan, and oak; many of them can be ordered by mail.

To complete your "Q" tool kit, you will need a long-handled spatula, fork, and tongs; a basting brush for saucing meats; and skewers and wire baskets for holding food that might otherwise slip through the grill rack into the fire. A thermometer is invaluable for testing the temperature of large roasts and smoked foods. You'll be familiar with most of the ingredients found in the Texas pantry, some of which are described below. For assistance in locating retail sources for unique ingredients and products, please call 1-800-526-2778.

Opposite:
City slickers and cowboy wanna-bes learn the basics of cooking outdoors at a dude ranch.
This page:
Old-fashioned coffee pots, such as this one, are ideal for outdoor use and are still frequently taken on camping trips.

Texas Ingredients

*A few usual and unusual products in
every well-stocked Texas pantry*

Pinto beans

Cactus paddles

Mexican cheese

AVOCADO: A leather-skinned fruit with rich, buttery flesh. The two most popular types are the California-grown Hass, a bumpy-skinned variety that turns black when ripe, and Florida's Fuerte, a larger, pear-shaped avocado with a thin, smooth green skin. To use, cut the avocado in half lengthwise, remove the pit, and scoop out the pulp from the skin. The pulp turns dark quickly upon exposure to the air. If you are not using it right away, return the pit to the hollow in the fruit or, if you have made guacamole, nest the pit in the center of it and seal well with plastic wrap, pressing the wrap directly onto the surface of the guacamole. An avocado is ripe when it yields slightly to gentle pressure. To ripen an avocado, put it on a countertop for a couple of days.

BEANS: Dried beans are staples in the Texas kitchen. Many varieties are used, including pinto, kidney, black beans, and black-eyed peas. Generally, all dried peas and beans need soaking except lentils, split peas, and black-eyed peas. Pick over the beans to remove any misshapen ones or any stones or grit, and rinse well. If soaking, place the beans in a pot and cover with several inches of water. Soak overnight (or quick-soak according to package directions). Drain the water, rinse the beans, and cover with cold water. Heat to boiling, then cover the pot and simmer for several hours until tender, adding water as necessary. Salt should be added after beans are soft. Canned beans can be substituted quite easily if they contain limited additional ingredients. Pinto beans or pink beans are the main ingredient in Tex-Mex refried beans, and baked beans of many varieties are incorporated into picnic and barbecue fare such as casseroles. Black-eyed peas are a southern specialty, finding their way into Texas "caviar" salad, and are considered to bring good luck if eaten on New Year's day. Red beans and rice are eaten in East Texas, and black beans are popular in soup and as a nacho ingredient.

CACTUS: Several cactus varieties with edible paddles and fruits exist; the prickly pear cactus is among the most common. The paddles (*nopales*) carry thorns, which must be carefully cut out with a knife. If you are lucky, you will find them sold already trimmed. Otherwise, grasp the paddles with a thick towel or wear a heavy glove. The paddles are generally cut into strips or cubes, boiled until tender, 5 to 10 minutes, and then rinsed well in cold water to remove any sliminess. They are cooked as a side dish; added to stews, scrambled eggs, and other dishes; or added raw to salads. The pear-shaped fruits, which are known as *tunas*, prickly pears, or cactus pears, have a sweet, fruity flavor and are used in fruit drinks, salads, and sorbets. They are available in cans, frozen, or fresh. The seeds of some varieties are hard and must be strained out.

CHEESE: A wide variety of cheese is used in the modern Texas kitchen, the more common varieties being Monterey Jack, Cheddar, Parmesan, Mozzarella, and Jalapeno Jack. Lesser-known fresh Mexican cheeses are also becoming more widely available and are worth experimenting with. Of all the cheeses, Monterey Jack is one of the most popular and is sold nationwide; it is a pale, semisoft California cheese with a mild flavor and excellent melting qualities.

CHILES: The heart and soul of Mexican, Tex-Mex, and Southwestern cooking are the chiles, which deliver the fire to countless dishes, such as chili, salsas, soups, tamales, and stews. Many types of both fresh and dried chiles are available, each with a unique flavor and a degree of heat that ranges from mild to searingly hot. Some chiles are also available canned, like green chiles (mild ancho chiles) and chipotles (smoked jalapeños), or pickled (jalapeños). The most commonly used fresh chiles are serrano, jalapeño, habañero (the hottest chile in North America), pequin, and poblano. The most popular dried chiles are ancho (mild) and chipotle (very hot). Jalapeños are round-shouldered, usually green but sometimes red, and are the most commonly found chile in the supermarkets. Another popular fresh chile is the fairly mild Anaheim chile, about 6 inches long. Anaheims are closely related to the New Mexico chile—which is also green and thick-fleshed—though the New Mexico is slightly longer, slimmer, and hotter. Aji chiles are very hot fresh chiles, found in both red and green state of ripeness, usually measuring 3 to 5 inches long and ¾ of an inch in diameter. The chile's intensity comes from the seeds and the interior rib membranes, so you may want to remove these before adding to dishes. If possible, wear thin rubber gloves when handling chiles to protect your skin from burning, and wash your hands thoroughly after working with them. Chiles can be stored in a paper bag in the refrigerator for about a week.

Chiles

CHILE POWDER: The most commonly used chile powder available in supermarkets is not actually pure chile powder, but a blend of chile pepper, cumin, oregano, salt, garlic, and other spices. Pure chile powder is sold in some supermarkets, specialty food stores, or whole-food markets. Pure chile powder can be mail-ordered, as well. In most recipes, the single-pepper powder or chile powder blends can be used interchangeably as "chile powder."

Chorizo

CHORIZO: This reddish, highly seasoned, coarsely ground pork or beef sausage is used in Spanish, Mexican, and Caribbean cooking. It is generally sold in links, sometimes vacuum packed. Many types are available, but all of them have paprika and garlic among their ingredients. Beef chorizo is less oily than pork chorizo. You can substitute any spicy sausage, although the flavor will be different.

Cilantro

Corn

Epazote

Hoja Santa

Jicama

Lemon thyme

CILANTRO: Also known as fresh coriander or Chinese parsley, cilantro is one of the most important herbs used in Texas and Tex-Mex cooking. It is the fresh leaf of the coriander plant, and although it resembles flat-leaf parsley, it has a more aromatic flavor. It is usually sold in small bunches. Look for ones with bright green leaves. Store as you would parsley.

CORN: A staple of Native Americans of the Southwest for centuries, corn is a versatile pantry item. The dried husks are softened with water and used to wrap tamales for a distinctive flavor. The corn kernels are eaten fresh off the cob, or used dried and ground into hominy, cornmeal, or made into *masa harina*, the dough flour used for making tortillas, tamales, corn bread, and grits. *Huitlachoche* is a fungus that attacks the growing ears of corn, causing the kernels to swell into a blue-grey mass. It's a prized specialty in Mexico and in recent years has been introduced to American palates. It is used in numerous dishes such as soups, stews, and stuffing mixtures.

CUMIN: This popular spice, a member of the parsley family, is one of the most aromatic flavorings used in the Tex-Mex kitchen. When a recipe calls for ground cumin, toast whole seeds in a dry pan and then grind them in a spice mill for the best flavor.

EPAZOTE: Also known as "wormseed" and "Mexican tea," this pungent herb grows wild in Mexico and parts of the United States. It is commonly used to flavor stews, meat, and bean dishes. Outside the southwestern states, epazote is available fresh in some city supermarkets, some specialty markets, as well as dried in most well-stocked supermarkets.

GRAPEFRUIT: Many varieties of citrus are grown in the Rio Grande Valley of Texas, but the red grapefruit cultivated there is famous around the world. The flesh varies from pink to light red color to dark red and the flesh is juicy and sweet. In the early part of the century, several pink to slightly reddish colored grapefruit were propagated into what is now known as the Ruby Red. In the late 1950s the Ruby Red was used to develop an ever darker red grapefruit that became known as the Rio Red. They're used interchangeably in recipes.

GRITS: A specialty of the South, grits is made from freshly ground, dried hulled corn kernels. It is typically boiled in water until thickened, and then served as a breakfast food or as a side dish.

HOJA SANTA: Literally named "holy leaf," this large-leaved, green herb has a taste reminiscent of a mixture of root beer and anise. It is used as a flavoring for soup, stews, and sauces, and for wrapping foods tamale-style and fish. It is stocked fresh in some markets in the Southwest. There is no true substitute.

JICAMA: Also known as yam bean, jicama (pronounced "HICKama") is an edible tuber native to Mexico, Central, and South America. The brown skin is inedible and should be removed; the white flesh is crisp, juicy, and sweet.

LEMON THYME: This lemon-scented thyme is a delightful species of thyme as it adds a lemony touch to poultry, meat and seafood dishes. It tends to lose its flavor fast when cooked though.

MEXICAN LIME: A small, fragrant, very tart, yellow-green lime that is also known as Key lime or West Indian lime. Smaller than most other lime varieties, you will need to substitute only one regular lime for every three Mexican limes called for in a recipe.

OREGANO: A small shrub with highly aromatic leaves. There are over thirty species of oregano, a herb of the marjoram family, of which Mexican oregano is a popular strain in the southern states and Mexico. Substitute any fresh or dried oregano for Mexican Oregano.

PIMENTO: The fruit of the red sweet Capsicum or bell pepper frequently used as a stuffing in olives and in Texas dishes.

POMEGRANATE: An autumn fruit grown primarily in the Middle East, although Texas, Arizona, and California now have small commercial crops. Inside the fruit are hundreds of pulp-covered seeds that are used for garnish or eaten as a snack. The pulp is made into a molasses that is available in Middle Eastern food stores and is used to flavor sauces. Be careful when working with pomegranates, as the juice stains are difficult to remove.

SWEET ONION: Texans are justly proud of their SpringSweet and 1015 SuperSweet Texas onions, grown in the South Texas Rio Grande Valley. They are juicy, due to their high water content, and have a sweet, mild character that causes little tearing when they are peeled and cut. The SpringSweets are available from mid-March through June, and the season of the larger 1015 SuperSweets is from mid-April through May. Buy onions with shiny, thin skins and tight, dry necks. They are readily available in supermarkets across the country. Store in a single layer in a well-ventilated area. If unavailable, substitute any mild onion.

TEQUILA: A liquor made exclusively in Mexico from the agave plant, tequila is the base for the margarita, tequila sunrise, and other cocktails. But the classic way to consume tequila is straight from a shot glass with salt and lime.

TORTILLA: The tortilla is a thin round of unleavened dough made from either corn or wheat flour. It is most commonly used to wrap foods, such as fillings for tacos, burritos, enchiladas, or fajitas. It also is filled with cheese or other ingredients and browned to make a quesadilla, or cut into wedges and deep-fried to make chips. Novices find tortillas difficult to make from scratch, but they are readily available in supermarkets throughout the country.

TOMATILLOS: Members of the gooseberry family, tomatillos look like unripe, green tomatoes. The thin, parchment-like husk encasing them is easily removed, and then they must be rinsed to remove the sticky residue that covers them. They are usually cooked to develop their flavor, although they are also used uncooked in salsas to add a sharp flavor. When buying tomatillos, select ones that are firm and have close-fitting husks. They also are available canned.

Mexican limes

Mexican oregano

Pomegranate

Tomatillos

Part Three: The Recipes

What's a snack in Texas could often be a whole meal almost anywhere else,
we begin with some snacks perfect for football watching

Texans are passionate about sports, especially football or, to be more precise, the Dallas Cowboys. Unless you're lucky enough to be sitting in the stands, not much can compete with watching the ball game on television with a bunch of friends and lots of snacks. Most of these can be made ahead of time except for the spicy, fried jalapeños that need to be cooked when you're ready to eat them so the batter is nice and crunchy. For the popcorn, add the melted butter at the last minute.

Chili Con Queso

2 tablespoons butter
1 medium-sized onion, chopped
3 jalapeño chiles, seeded and minced
$\frac{1}{4}$ cup roasted red pepper, chopped
3 garlic cloves, minced
2 medium tomatoes, seeded and chopped
2 cups shredded Monterey Jack cheese, or a mix of Monterey and Longhorn cheese
2 cups shredded Cheddar cheese
$\frac{1}{2}$ teaspoon cayenne pepper
$\frac{1}{2}$ teaspoon black pepper
$\frac{1}{4}$ teaspoon chile powder
$\frac{1}{2}$ teaspoon paprika
$\frac{1}{4}$ teaspoon salt
$\frac{1}{2}$ cup half-and-half
1 tablespoon all-purpose flour
Tortilla chips

In a large skillet, melt the butter over medium heat. Add the onions and sauté until tender, about 2 to 3 minutes. Add the jalapeño chiles, roasted pepper, garlic, and tomatoes and continue to cook over medium heat until the vegetables are tender and the tomatoes have released their juices, about 10 minutes. (The recipe can be prepared to this point up to 3 days ahead, cooled, covered, and refrigerated. Gently reheat when ready to use.) Stir in the cheese, spices, and $\frac{1}{4}$ teaspoon salt.

In a small bowl, mix together the half-and-half and flour and slowly stir into the cheese mixture. Continue to heat, stirring occasionally, until the cheese is fully melted. Serve warm with tortilla chips. Yields about $2\frac{1}{2}$ cups.

Tomatillo Salsa

$\frac{3}{4}$ pound (about 6) tomatillos, husks removed and quartered
1 jalapeño chile, seeded and coarsely chopped
$\frac{1}{4}$ cup chopped onion
2 garlic cloves, crushed
$\frac{1}{4}$ cup packed fresh cilantro leaves
1 tablespoon fresh lime juice
2 teaspoons olive oil
$\frac{3}{4}$ teaspoon salt

Combine all ingredients in a blender and process until smooth. Pour into a bowl and serve immediately, or cover and refrigerate for up to 2 days. Serve with tortilla chips. Yields about $1\frac{1}{2}$ cups.

Opposite:
(clockwise from top left) Fried Jalapeños, Nacho Popcorn, Fresh Tomato Salsa, Tomatillo Salsa, and Chili con Queso.

Pickled Okra

2 pounds tender okra
1 small onion, sliced
18 whole garlic cloves, peeled
6 teaspoons peppercorns
1 teaspoon mustard seeds
24 or more, small, hot chiles
6 sprigs fresh dill
6 cups white vinegar
4 1/2 tablespoons sugar
3 tablespoons salt

Wash the okra and remove the stem tips. Sterilize six glass pint-sized jars. Place some onion, and a third of the garlic, peppercorns, mustard seeds and hot chiles in the bottom of each hot jar. Place a row of okra in each jar, standing upright against the outer edge, with stems pointing down. Tipping the jar sideways makes this a little easier. Slide a sprig of dill between the okra and the glass of each jar and add an additional third of the seasonings. The seasonings should be placed so that they can be seen from outside of the jar. Add another row of okra, this time with the stem end facing upward. The rows of okra should interlock. Continue to add the okra until the jars are filled. Sprinkle with the remaining seasonings.

In a large pot, combine the vinegar, sugar, and salt and bring to a boil. Immediately pour the vinegar mixture over the okra, filling to $\frac{1}{2}$ inch from the top. Clean the rim of the jars and seal immediately. Let the okra stand for two weeks before serving. The okra is crisper if served chilled. Yields about 6 pints.

Fresh Tomato Salsa

2 pounds tomatoes, seeded and chopped
$\frac{3}{4}$ cup chopped onion
$\frac{1}{4}$ cup chopped fresh cilantro
2 garlic cloves, minced
1 jalapeño chile, seeded and finely chopped
2 tablespoons fresh lime juice
$1\frac{1}{2}$ teaspoons salt

Combine all of the ingredients in a large bowl. Stir until thoroughly mixed. Cover and refrigerate for at least 30 minutes, but no longer than a day ahead before serving. Serve warm or chilled with tortilla chips. Yields about 3 cups.

Guacamole

2 ripe Hass avocados
$1\frac{1}{2}$ jalapeño chiles, seeded and minced,
  or to taste
2 small tomatoes, seeded and chopped
2 tablespoons minced onion
1 tablespoon fresh lime juice
2 tablespoons minced fresh cilantro
Tortilla chips

Put the avocados into a mixing bowl and mash with a fork, leaving bits of avocado for texture. Add the remaining ingredients except the tortilla chips, then adjust seasoning to taste.

Serve immediately with tortilla chips, or cover, pressing plastic wrap directly onto the surface, and refrigerate for up to 30 minutes. Yields about $1\frac{1}{2}$ cups.

Nacho Popcorn

10 cups (2$\frac{1}{2}$ quarts) freshly popped popcorn
1 teaspoon paprika
$\frac{3}{4}$ teaspoon chile powder
$\frac{3}{4}$ teaspoon ground cumin
4 tablespoons butter, melted
$\frac{1}{2}$ cup grated Parmesan cheese
Salt to taste

Put the popped corn into a large serving bowl. Sprinkle the paprika, chile powder, and cumin over the popcorn and toss to mix. Pour the melted butter over the top and then sprinkle with the Parmesan cheese. Toss well again. Serve warm. Yields 10 cups.

Texas Caviar Salad

3 cups cooked black-eyed peas, drained
1/3 cup finely chopped yellow bell pepper
1/3 cup finely chopped red bell pepper
1/4 cup finely chopped onion
1/2 cup finely chopped celery
1 garlic clove, minced
2 serrano chiles, finely chopped
2 tablespoons olive oil
1/4 cup red wine vinegar
1 tablespoon balsamic vinegar
1 tablespoon chopped fresh cilantro
1/4 teaspoon ground cumin
1/2 teaspoon salt
1/2 teaspoon freshly ground pepper

In a bowl, combine all of the ingredients and mix well. Cover and refrigerate for 3 to 4 hours before serving. Serve chilled as a side dish. Makes 4 cups.

Fried Jalapenos

12 jalapeño chiles, of uniform size
$\frac{1}{2}$ pound Mozzarella cheese, shredded
$\frac{1}{4}$ cup chopped pimento
1 tablespoon chopped fresh parsley
1 teaspoon salt
$\frac{1}{4}$ teaspoon ground cumin
1 cup cornmeal
1$\frac{1}{2}$ cups all-purpose flour
$\frac{1}{4}$ teaspoon baking powder
1 cup milk
Vegetable oil for frying

Make a length-wise slit along one side of each jalapeño. Carefully remove the seeds and the membrane. Do not remove the stem. Set the chiles aside.

In a small bowl, toss together the Mozzarella cheese, pimento, parsley, and $\frac{1}{4}$ teaspoon of the salt. In a large bowl, combine the cumin, cornmeal, flour, baking powder, the remaining $\frac{3}{4}$ teaspoon salt, and the milk. Stir to form a batter free from lumps. Fill the chiles with the cheese mixture, dividing it evenly.

Pour oil to a depth of 3 inches into a deep pan and heat to 360° F. Holding a chile by the stem, dip it into the batter until it is coated completely, then carefully drop it into the oil. Repeat with the remaining chiles, cooking one layer at a time. Fry until golden brown, then transfer to paper towels to drain. Serve immediately. Yields 12 chiles, enough for 3 or 4 people.

POTATO-CRUSTED FRIED CALAMARI

Michael Cordua, Américas, Houston

These crispy calamari strips, which are also known as tiritas, are sparked with two spicy dips. They are guaranteed to be among the first snacks to disappear at your next cocktail party. Serve them piping hot for best results.

Jalapeño Mayonnaise

2 cups mayonnaise
Juice of 1 lime
Salt and freshly ground pepper to taste
2 tablespoons diced onion
2 tablespoons diced red bell pepper
1 jalapeño chile, seeded and diced
2 tablespoons diced green onion
2 tablespoons chopped cilantro

Spicy Ketchup

2 cups ketchup
$1/2$ teaspoon cayenne pepper, or to taste
Juice of $1^1/_2$ limes

Calamari

$1^1/_4$ pounds cleaned squid
Salt and freshly ground black pepper taste
$1^1/_2$ cups all-purpose flour
$1^1/_2$ cups egg wash ($1^1/_4$ cups beaten egg mixed with $1/4$ cup water)
10 ounces potato chips, crushed into small pieces
Peanut oil for frying

To make the **jalapeño mayonnaise**, combine the mayonnaise, lime juice, salt, and pepper in a bowl and mix well. Fold in the remaining ingredients, cover, and chill.

To make the **spicy ketchup**, combine all the ingredients and mix well. Cover and chill.

To make the **calamari**, pour peanut oil to a depth of 3 inches into a deep pan and heat to 375°F. While the oil is heating, cut the squid bodies lengthwise into strips $1/4$-inch wide and season with salt and pepper. Toss the strips in flour and then dip them in the egg wash, allowing the excess to drip off. Finally, toss the strips in the crushed potato chips. Working in batches, deep-fry the calamari until golden, about 3 minutes. Transfer to paper towels to drain.

Serve immediately with the jalapeño mayonnaise and spicy ketchup. Serves 6.

BLACK BEAN-MONTASIO CHEESE NACHOS

Dean Fearing, The Mansion on Turtle Creek, Dallas

Just the mention of nachos makes a Texan's mouth water, and not surprisingly, a multitude of variations exist on this popular local dish. This recipe combines Gulf shrimp and black beans, with the crunch of jicama. Mild, sweet Texas onions are part of the tasty mix, although any other mild onion can be substituted. Use Romano cheese if Montasio is unavailable.

Jicama Salsa

- 12 large shrimp (10–15 count per pound), peeled and deveined
- Salt
- 1 tablespoon minced garlic
- 3 tablespoons minced jalapeño chile, seeded if desired
- $\frac{1}{3}$ cup minced sweet Texas onion
- $\frac{1}{2}$ cup avocado ($\frac{1}{4}$-inch dice)
- $\frac{1}{2}$ cup diced jicama ($\frac{1}{4}$-inch dice)
- $\frac{1}{3}$ cup diced red tomato ($\frac{1}{4}$-inch dice)
- $\frac{1}{3}$ cup diced yellow tomato ($\frac{1}{4}$-inch dice)
- 1 tablespoon grated ginger
- 2 tablespoons chopped fresh cilantro
- 1 tablespoon chopped fresh basil
- 3 tablespoons fresh lime juice
- 3 tablespoons extra-virgin olive oil

- 1 cup drained, cooked black beans, puréed to make a paste
- 24 triangular tortilla chips
- $\frac{1}{3}$ cup grated Montasio cheese

To make the **jicama salsa**, prepare a medium-hot grill. Season the shrimp with salt and place over the hot fire. Grill, turning as needed, until cooked through, about 3 minutes. Remove from the grill, let cool, and chop. In a bowl, combine the shrimp and all the remaining ingredients and mix well. Season to taste with salt.

Spread each tortilla with black bean purée and arrange on a platter. Sprinkle liberally with the Montasio cheese and top with salsa. Serves 8 to 10.

CEVICHE COPACABANA

Michael Cordua, Américas, Houston

Ceviche (or seviche) is raw fish or other seafood that has been marinated or "cooked" in citrus juices, usually lemon or lime, and flavored with herbs and spices. It is a popular Latin American dish that requires the freshest seafood available.

- **1 pound very small shrimp, peeled and deveined**
- **1 pound firm whitefish fillets such as corvina (sea bass) or grouper, cut into $\frac{1}{2}$-inch cubes**
- **Juice of 12 bitter oranges, or juice of 8 lemons and 8 limes**
- **4 ají or jalapeño chiles, finely chopped, seeded if desired**
- **2 large red onions, very thinly sliced**
- **Salt and freshly ground pepper to taste**
- **1 cup chopped fresh cilantro**
- **1 tablespoon tiny capers**

Garnish

- **4 small hearts of romaine lettuce, shredded**
- **12 stalks heart of palm**
- **1 mango, peeled and slivered**
- **$\frac{1}{2}$ red bell pepper, thinly sliced**
- **1 Hass avocado, peeled and diced**

To make the ceviche, drop the shrimp into boiling water and cook for 1 minute. Remove immediately from the water and put into ice water to stop the cooking. In a bowl, mix together the shrimp, fish, citrus juice, chiles, onions, salt, and pepper. Cover and refrigerate for 4 hours. Check the fish for doneness: it should be opaque throughout and flake easily.

To serve, mix the cilantro and capers into the ceviche. Place some romaine in the bottom of each serving bowl or plate. Top with some of the ceviche, heart of palm, mango, red bell pepper and avocado. Serves 6.

FIESTA CLAMS

Bruce Molzan, Ruggles Grill, Houston

The Gulf Coast supplies the shellfish for this clam recipe, though oysters can be substituted. A great party dish, this attractive appetizer can be doubled and served as a main course. The apples served alongside are filled with pico de gallo.

Pico de Gallo

4 Granny Smith or other tart apples
1 cup plus $\frac{1}{4}$ cup fresh lemon juice
4 large tomatoes, diced
1 medium red onion, diced
1 jalapeño chile, seeded and diced
1 bunch fresh cilantro, chopped
Salt and freshly ground pepper to taste

Clams

24 large clams in the shell
$\frac{1}{4}$ cup fresh lemon juice
$\frac{1}{4}$ cup white wine
Salt and freshly ground pepper
1 cup shredded Monterey Jack cheese
$\frac{1}{2}$ cup diced red bell pepper
$\frac{1}{2}$ cup diced yellow bell pepper
4 green onions (white and green parts), chopped
8 slices bacon, half-cooked, cut into $\frac{1}{2}$-inch pieces

To prepare the **pico de gallo**, cut a $\frac{1}{2}$-inch slice off the stem end of each apple, reserving the tops. With a paring knife or serrated grapefruit spoon, scoop out the core from each apple and hollow out the pulp to form a cavity with sturdy sides. Reserve the pulp for another use. Soak the apples in the 1 cup of lemon juice to prevent darkening. Turn the apples over to drain any remaining lemon juice into a mixing bowl. To the bowl, add the tomatoes, onion, jalapeño, cilantro, the $\frac{1}{4}$ cup of lemon juice, salt, and pepper. Spoon the mixture into the apples and replace the tops.

To prepare the **clams**, preheat the oven to 375°F. Rinse the clams well, scrubbing the shells with a stiff-bristled brush. Bring a saucepan filled with salted water to a boil, drop in the clams, and boil 2 to 4 minutes. Remove immediately with a slotted utensil and allow to cool to room temperature for 15 minutes. Pull off and discard the top shells. With a paring knife, cut the clam muscle to free the meat from the bottom shell of each clam, leaving the meat on the shell. Put the clams with their shells on a baking sheet, and sprinkle the lemon juice, wine, salt, and pepper evenly over the clams. Top the clams with the cheese, red and yellow peppers, green onions, and bacon.

Bake until the bacon is crisp and the cheese is melted, 5 to 6 minutes. Serve immediately, accompanied by the filled apples. Serves 4.

1000 SPICE FRIED QUAIL

Danielle Custer, Laurels, Westin Park Central Hotel, Dallas

Marinate the quail and make the potato–white bean purée the day before you plan to serve them, but prepare the black-eyed pea relish and the Garlic–red Chile Oil on the day they will be used. If you like highly spiced dishes, the Garlic–red Chile Oil is for you. Otherwise, use it sparingly. This dish can be expanded and served as a main course. It also works well with Cornish hens or small frying chickens.

6 semi boneless quail, cut in half along the breast
1 cup each finely chopped watercress and arugula

Breast Marinade

Juice of 2 lemons
1/4 cup soy sauce
2 teaspoons chopped garlic
1 teaspoon fresh-ground black pepper
1 teaspoon paprika
1/2 teaspoon ground red pepper

Back Marinade

1/2 cup hot-pepper sauce
1 teaspoon fresh-ground black pepper
1 teaspoon paprika

Fried Quail

3 cups canola oil
2 cups all-purpose flour
2 tablespoons freshly ground pepper
1 tablespoon salt

Potato–White Bean Purée (see recipe, page 127)
Black-eyed Pea Relish (see recipe, page 128)
Garlic-red Chile Oil (see recipe, page 134)

Prepare the **breast marinade** and **back marinade** by combining the ingredients for each into small bowls. At least 1 day before serving, lay the quail, breast-side up, in a large glass or stainless-steel baking pan and rub in the breast marinade. Flip the birds over and do the same on their backs with the back marinade. Cover and refrigerate.

To prepare the **fried quail**, pour 1 inch of canola oil into a large, deep pan and heat to 350°F. While the oil is heating, mix together the flour, pepper, and salt in a shallow bowl or pie plate. Coat both sides of the split quail in the flour mixture. Add 3 or 4 pieces to the hot oil and fry, turning once, until browned, 2 to 3 minutes on each side. Transfer with tongs or a slotted spoon to paper towels to drain; keep warm. Repeat with the remaining pieces.

To serve, spread one-sixth of the **potato–white bean purée** on the bottom of a large salad plate. Toss the watercress and arugula with a little of the **black-eyed pea relish** for dressing, then put one-sixth of the remaining relish on top of the bean purée. Sprinkle with one-sixth of the watercress and arugula. Place 2 hot fried quail halves on top of the beans and sprinkle the edge of the plate with **garlic-red chile oil**. Repeat to assemble 5 more plates. Serve immediately. Serves 6.

TORTILLA SOUP

Dean Fearing, The Mansion on Turtle Creek, Dallas

Tortilla soup is a Southwestern classic, and probably the most popular soup in Texas. It's basically chicken soup that has been glorified with tomatoes, interesting Mexican spices, herbs, and chile peppers. Fried tortilla strips garnish the soup along with avocado cubes and shredded cheese. It's hearty enough to serve as a meal. If you're not going to serve it right away, make the soup ahead of time and add the garnishes at the last minute.

3 tablespoons corn oil
4 corn tortillas, cut into long strips
8 garlic cloves, peeled
2 cups fresh onion purée
4 cups fresh tomato purée
5 dried New Mexican green chiles
   (or Anaheim chile)
2 jalapeños chiles, chopped
1 tablespoon ground cumin
1 tablespoon chopped epazote
   (or 2 tablespoons chopped fresh cilantro)
1 teaspoon ground coriander
1 large bay leaf
1½ quarts chicken stock
Salt to taste
Lemon juice to taste
Cayenne pepper to taste (optional)

Garnish

1 cooked, whole, skinless, boneless chicken
   breast, cut into thin strips
1 large avocado, peeled, seeded and cut into
   small cubes
1½ cups shredded Cheddar cheese
4 corn tortillas, cut into thin strips and fried
   crisp

To make the **tortilla soup**, heat the oil in a large saucepan over medium heat. Add the tortillas and garlic and sauté until the tortillas are crisp and the garlic is golden brown, about 4 to 5 minutes. Add the onion purée and cook for 5 minutes, stirring occasionally until reduced by half. Add the tomato purée, chiles, jalapeños, cumin, epazote, coriander, bay leaf and chicken stock. Bring to a boil. Lower the heat and simmer for approximately 40 minutes. Skim the fat from the surface if necessary. Process through a food mill to attain the perfect consistency or use a blender. If the soup becomes too thick, thin with some additional chicken stock. Season to taste with salt, lemon juice and optional cayenne.

Ladle the soup into warm bowls. Garnish each bowl equally with portions of chicken breast, avocado, shredded cheese and crisp tortilla strips. Serve immediately. Serves 4 to 6.

RED-HOT VENISON CHILI

Also called *chili con carne,* this is a variation of the thick soup traditionally made with highly seasoned ground beef and chiles. Proclaimed the state dish by the Texas legislature in 1977, it is one of the most famous local preparations and the topic of many heated conversations over ingredients and whether beans or tomatoes should be included. Recipes for chili date back to the mid-1800s, when a "bowl of red" was basic fare. Today, it can be a passion. If you're not a devotee of beans in chili, simply omit them. The fry bread is typical of the fried dough cooked by Native Americans for centuries.

Chili

- 2 tablespoons vegetable oil
- 1 large onion, finely chopped
- 1 bell pepper, finely chopped
- 6 garlic cloves, minced
- 2 pounds ground venison
- 2 jalapeño chiles, minced, or to taste
- 1 tablespoon plus 1 teaspoon chile powder
- $3/4$ teaspoon cayenne pepper
- $2^1/_2$ teaspoons ground cumin
- 1 tablespoon dried oregano
- 1 ($15^1/_2$-ounce) can red kidney beans, drained
- 1 (28-ounce) can crushed tomatoes
- 1 (6-ounce) can tomato paste
- $3^1/_2$ cups beef stock
- $1^1/_2$ teaspoons salt

Indian Fry Bread

- 2 cups all-purpose flour
- 2 teaspoons baking powder
- $1/2$ teaspoon salt
- 2 tablespoons solid vegetable shortening
- 1 cup milk
- Vegetable oil for frying

Heat the oil in a skillet over medium-high heat. Sauté the onion, bell pepper, and garlic until tender. Add the venison and cook through, breaking up the ground meat. Drain any liquid. Stir in the remaining ingredients. Bring to a boil, reduce the heat, and simmer, uncovered, for about 2 hours. Stir occasionally. Adjust the seasonings.

To make the **fry bread,** sift together the flour, baking powder, and salt. Cut the shortening into the flour. Add the milk and stir to form a ball.

Knead the dough on a floured surface for about 3 minutes, until the flour is incorporated and the dough is smooth. Dust with flour if the dough feels tacky. Divide into 8 equal pieces, roll into balls, and put back into the bowl. Cover and let rest for 30 minutes.

On a floured surface, roll out each ball into a round about $1/8$ inch thick. Cut a quarter-sized hole in the center of each round.

Heat 1 inch of oil in a deep pan to 370°F. In batches, add the rounds and fry, until golden brown, about $1^1/_2$ minutes on each side. Transfer to paper towels to drain.

Serve the chili and fry bread piping hot. Makes about 8 cups of chili and 8 pieces of fry bread.

ROASTED ACORN SQUASH SOUP

Danielle Custer, Laurels, Westin Park Central Hotel, Dallas

In the fall, markets are flooded with acorn squash, and many cooks like to turn these seasonal vegetables into wonderful soups. This recipe is easy, and it makes a delicious lunch or first course. The sage pesto and the brown sugar glaze can be made up to 2 days ahead of time. This soup freezes well.

Bourbon–Brown Sugar Glaze
  7 tablespoons brown sugar
  $\frac{1}{4}$ cup bourbon
  $\frac{1}{2}$ cup ($\frac{1}{4}$ pound) butter

Soup
  1 ($1\frac{1}{2}$-pound) acorn squash
  6 tablespoons butter
  1 cup finely chopped onion
  $\frac{1}{3}$ cup finely chopped carrot
  $\frac{1}{4}$ cup white wine
  $\frac{3}{4}$ cup peeled, diced potato
  $2\frac{1}{2}$ cups chicken stock
  Salt and freshly ground pepper to taste
  Fresh lemon juice to taste

  Sage Pesto (see recipe, page 138)

To make the **bourbon–brown sugar glaze**, combine the brown sugar and bourbon in a saucepan over medium heat and reduce until a paste starts to form. Whisk in the butter until it is fully incorporated. Keep hot or reheat in a double boiler. If the mixture separates during reheating, put the mixture in the blender for a few seconds to bind. Reserve.

To make the **soup**, preheat the oven to 400°F. Cut the squash in half and scoop out and discard the seeds. Place, hollow side up, in a baking pan and place 2 tablespoons of the butter in the center of each half. Cover and roast until tender, about an hour and 15 minutes. Remove from the oven and, when cool enough to handle, scoop out the pulp and reserve.

In a large pot, melt the remaining 2 tablespoons butter over medium heat. Add the onion and carrot and sauté until tender. Deglaze the pan with the wine, stirring to dislodge any browned bits. Add the potatoes, squash pulp, and stock and bring to a boil. Reduce the heat to low and simmer, uncovered, until the potatoes are tender, about 10 minutes. In batches, purée the soup in the blender until smooth. Return the soup to the pot and season to taste with salt, pepper, and lemon juice.

To serve, spoon the hot soup into bowls and drizzle with the sage pesto and brown sugar glaze. Yields about 4 cups. Serves 3 to 4.

EL PASO SALPICON

In the West Texas city of El Paso, spicy shredded brisket of beef salad is a specialty. After the brisket is cooked in a flavorful broth, it is very finely shredded and mixed with chile-spiked dressing and Monterey Jack cheese. Garnished with avocado, red onion slices and tomato wedges, the brisket is served with warm tortillas. Some diners may roll up the brisket like a burrito.

1 (3-pound) beef brisket
1 onion, roughly chopped
1 carrot, quartered
1 celery rib, cut into quarters
2 garlic cloves, chopped
$\frac{1}{2}$ cup packed fresh cilantro leaves
2 (14-ounce) cans beef broth, or $3\frac{1}{2}$ cups water
1 (28-ounce) can crushed tomatoes
Salt to taste
$\frac{1}{2}$ cup olive oil
$\frac{1}{4}$ cup white wine vinegar
$\frac{1}{4}$ cup fresh lime juice
1 (7-ounce) can chipotle chiles in adobo,
    or 1 (4-ounce) can chopped green chiles,
    puréed, or to taste
Salt and freshly ground pepper to taste
$\frac{1}{2}$ pound Monterey Jack cheese, cubed

Garnish

1 head romaine lettuce, separated into leaves
2 tomatoes, cut into wedges
1 small red onion, thinly sliced
2 ripe avocados, sliced lengthwise and tossed in
    fresh lemon juice
1 green onion (white and green parts) sliced
Tortillas, warmed

Put the brisket, fatty side up, in a heavy, 4-quart pot. Add the onion, carrot, celery, garlic, cilantro, broth or water, and tomatoes. Cover and bring to a boil, then reduce the heat to low and simmer until the brisket is very tender and shreds easily when pierced with a fork, about 3 hours. Add more broth or water if needed to keep the brisket covered during cooking. Season with salt.

Remove the brisket and reserve the broth for another use. When still warm, but cool enough to handle, use a fork to shred the brisket as finely as possible. It should have a light, cottonlike texture. Toss it with a little of the broth to keep it moist.

In a large bowl, combine the olive oil, vinegar, lime juice, and some of the chiles. Add the shredded brisket and toss to mix. Taste and increase the amount of chiles to taste. Adjust the seasonings with salt and pepper. Just before serving, add all but a handful of the cheese and toss again to mix. Reserve the remaining cheese for garnish.

To serve, line a platter with the lettuce leaves and mound the brisket in the center. Surround the brisket with the tomato wedges, onion slices, and avocado slices. Sprinkle the green onions and the reserved cheese over the top. Serve with the tortillas. Serves 8 to 10.

HUEVOS RANCHEROS

Once upon a time, huevos rancheros was a hearty dish served for breakfast only. But no more. Now it's so popular that it is eaten for brunch, lunch, and even dinner. Serve refried beans alongside.

4 (6-inch) tortillas
2 tablespoons olive oil
$^{3}/_{4}$ cup coarsely chopped onion
$^{1}/_{2}$ cup coarsely chopped green bell pepper
1 garlic clove, minced
1 cup seeded, chopped tomato
1 tablespoon minced jalapeño chile
4 teaspoons chile powder
$^{1}/_{4}$ teaspoon ground cumin
$^{1}/_{2}$ teaspoon salt
$^{1}/_{4}$ teaspoon freshly ground pepper
8 eggs

Garnish: fresh cilantro sprigs

Preheat an oven to 200°F. Wrap the tortillas in aluminum foil and place in the oven to warm. Also place 4 ovenproof plates in the oven.

In a skillet, heat 1 tablespoon of the olive oil over medium heat. Add the onion, bell pepper, and garlic. Sauté until tender, about 4 minutes. Add the tomato, chile, chile powder, cumin, salt, pepper, and $^{1}/_{4}$ cup water. Stir well and continue to cook over medium heat for about 5 minutes. Remove the sauce from the heat and keep warm.

In a large skillet, heat the remaining tablespoon of olive oil over medium heat and fry the eggs. Meanwhile, remove the tortillas from the oven, take them out of the foil, and put one warmed tortilla on each of the warmed plates. Place 2 fried eggs on each tortilla, then spoon about one-fourth of the Ranchero sauce over the eggs. Garnish with cilantro sprigs. Serve immediately. Serves 4.

TEXAS SWEET ONION PIE

Texas sweet onions are mild, juicy, and exceptionally sweet, similar in taste to Georgia's Vidalia onions, Hawaii's Maui onions, and Washington's Walla Walla onions. Although these sweet spheres are popular cooked or uncooked as a topping for burgers or in salsas or salads, some people love a simple sandwich of thinly sliced onion tucked between two thin pieces of bread smeared with a bit of mayonnaise. Cooking the onions in a pie—a throwback to the days of quiche—brings out their gentle flavor and makes a perfect lunch or brunch dish. The pie freezes well, so make two and keep one for another day. Sweet onions are available in supermarkets in the spring.

3 tablespoons butter
4 cups thinly sliced Texas sweet onions
1 cup milk
1 teaspoon salt
4 teaspoons all-purpose flour
1 teaspoon chile powder
$\frac{1}{2}$ pound Monterey Jack cheese, grated
3 eggs
1 9-inch deep-dish pie shell, unbaked

Preheat the oven to 350° F. In a sauté pan, melt the butter over medium heat. Add the onions and sauté until tender, about 8-10 minutes. Meanwhile, put the milk and salt in a saucepan over medium heat to scald, then set aside to cool.

In a bowl, stir together the flour and the chile powder, then add the cheese and toss to mix.

In another bowl, whisk the eggs until blended, then stir them into the scalded milk. Add the cheese mixture and mix well.

Drain any liquid from the sautéed onions and spoon them into the pie shell. Pour the egg-and-cheese mixture over the onions to fill the pie shell. Bake until a knife inserted into the center comes out clean, about 40 minutes. Remove from the oven and cool on a rack. Serve warm. Serves 8.

KOLACHES

During the latter half of the nineteenth century, many Czechs emigrated to Texas, arriving through the port of Galveston, and bringing with them culinary traditions that remain intact today. Along with homemade sausages, sauerkraut, and strudels, kolaches may be added to the list. They're delightful yeast pastries, similar to the Danish-style pastry we know and love, filled with fruit, poppy seed, or crumb toppings, while some encase sausage or cream cheese concoctions. Kolache bakeries and shops turn them out every day and Caldwell, the kolache capital of the world, holds an annual festival and cook-off. These are best eaten the day they are made. Filling made from soaked and mashed or puréed dried fruit works best, because jam tends to run over the sides. Or sprinkle them with powdered sugar when cool.

$1/4$ cup warm water (105–115°F)
1 package dry yeast
1 cup milk
2 tablespoons sugar
1 egg
2 tablespoons butter
2 tablespoons vegetable shortening
$1/2$ teaspoon salt
$2 1/2$–3 cups flour

Place the warm water in a small bowl and sprinkle in the yeast to dissolve. In a small saucepan scald the milk. Remove from the heat and cool to 80°F. Add the sugar, egg, butter, and shortening. Add the yeast mixture and mix well. Transfer to a large bowl. Add the salt and the flour 1 cup at a time, working it in thoroughly after each addition. It will be slightly sticky. Turn the dough onto a lightly floured board, and gently knead a few minutes until smooth. Put in a greased bowl and cover with a damp cloth until the dough has doubled, $1 1/2$ to 2 hours. Meanwhile, line a baking sheet. Punch down the dough in the bowl and knead slightly. Roll the dough into 20 to 24 large, smooth balls and place on the sheet pan, 2 inches apart. Or, roll out the dough and cut with a biscuit cutter or other shaped cutter. Let the dough rise again for 25 to 35 minutes. Make an indention in the center of each kolache and fill with a slice of sausage or a teaspoon of puréed fruit.

Bake at 375°F for 15 minutes or until golden. Remove from the oven and transfer the kolaches to a wire rack to cool. Yields 20 to 24 kolaches.

HUBCAP HAMBURGERS & HUGE ONION RINGS

Texans, like many others, consider the hamburger their own, insisting it was invented in the Lone Star State in the early 1900s. But ask a dozen different local cooks the secret to a perfect hamburger, and you'll get a dozen different answers.

Add a huge pile of fried onion rings and a chilled beer or a big glass of iced tea and your day is just about made.

HUBCAP HAMBURGERS

2 pounds ground chuck, preferably freshly ground
Salt and freshly ground pepper
$1/2$ pound Cheddar cheese, thinly sliced
4 hamburger buns, split
Mayonnaise
Mustard (optional)
4 lettuce leaves
4 tomato slices
4 onion slices, preferably sweet Texas, each about $3/8$ -inch thick

Divide the meat into 4 equal portions, and shape each portion into a thick patty. Handle the beef as little as possible to keep the coarse grind. Season each patty with salt and pepper.

Prepare a grill, or heat a cast-iron skillet over medium-high heat. Place the hamburgers on the grill or in the skillet and cook, turning once, until cooked through, about 5 minutes on each side.

Meanwhile, heat the hamburger buns, cut side down, on the grill for 1 to 2 minutes, or put them in a warm oven to heat for a few minutes. About 1 minute before the burgers are done, top them with the cheese slices, cover, and allow to melt.

Spread the hamburger buns with mayonnaise and mustard, if desired. Remove the hamburgers from the grill and place a patty on one side of each bun. Top with lettuce, tomato, and onion. Cover with the other half of the bun and serve immediately with the fried onion rings. Serves 4.

HUGE ONION RINGS

2 large sweet Texas onions
1 egg
$1^{1}/_{2}$ cups flour
$1/2$ cup buttermilk
12 ounces beer
2 tablespoons peanut oil
2 teaspoons salt
1 teaspoon freshly ground black pepper
Peanut oil for frying

Peel the onions and slice in $3/4$-inch rings. Remove the medium to large rings and set aside. Discard the centers of the onions or reserve for another use. Lightly beat the egg in a large mixing bowl. Whisk in the remaining ingredients until mixture is smooth.

Heat about 2 inches of oil in a large frying pan to 375°F. Dip the onion rings into the batter and carefully drop into the hot oil. Fry one layer at a time until lightly browned. Drain on paper towels. Keep warm in a 200°F oven until the hamburgers are cooked. Serve immediately. Serves 6.

PORK ASADO

Grady Spears, Reata Restaurants, Alpine/Fort Worth

Texans who hunger for a real breakfast are not satisfied with toast and a cup of coffee. They want plates filled with eggs, bacon, sausage, Huevos Rancheros (see recipe, page 56), even pork chops or steak. This recipe from West Texas is delicious served alongside eggs or as a taco filling.

Red Chile Paste
  2 ancho chiles, seeded and stemmed
  2 dried New Mexico or guajillo chiles, seeded
  1$\frac{1}{2}$ cups chicken stock
  $\frac{1}{4}$ white onion, chopped
  2 small garlic cloves, minced

Red Chile Sauce
  2 cups Red Chile Paste
  1 cup diced tomato
  1 teaspoon ground cumin
  1 tablespoon honey
  Kosher salt to taste
  2 tablespoons vegetable oil

Pork
  $\frac{1}{2}$ cup all-purpose flour
  Kosher salt to taste
  4 pounds pork butt, cut into $\frac{1}{2}$-inch cubes
  2 tablespoons oil
  1 cup diced bacon
  $\frac{1}{2}$ cup diced red onion
  6 garlic cloves, coarsely chopped
  2 cups red chile sauce
  2 cups chicken stock

To make the **chile paste**, put the chiles in a saucepan, add the chicken stock, and bring to a boil over high heat. Reduce the heat to low and simmer until the peppers are soft, about 15 minutes. Pour the contents of the pan into a blender and process on low speed until puréed. You should have about 2 cups of paste.

To make the **chile sauce**, put the 2 cups chile paste, the tomato, cumin, and honey in a blender and process until smooth. Season with salt. In a skillet, heat the oil over medium-high heat. Pour in the purée and cook for 3 minutes to blend the flavors. Measure out 2 cups and reserve the remaining sauce for another use.

To make the **pork**, combine the flour and the salt in a bowl. Toss the pork in the flour and shake off the excess. In a large Dutch oven or deep skillet, heat the oil over medium heat. Add the bacon, onion, and garlic and sauté until the onion is translucent but not browned, 4 to 5 minutes. Raise the heat to medium-high, add the floured pork cubes, and cook, turning as necessary, until well browned on all sides. Add the 2 cups chile sauce and the chicken stock, reduce the heat and simmer until the pork is tender, 25 to 30 minutes. Serve hot. Serves 6 to 8.

CANDIED PECAN SNAPPER

Bruce Molzan, Ruggles Grill, Houston

Over two hundred varieties of this firm-fleshed fish exist, fifteen of which are found in the southern Atlantic waters from North Carolina throughout the Gulf of Mexico. Rice with sun-dried tomatoes or apricots is good served alongside the fish.

Candied Pecan Snapper, served with rice and sun-dried tomatoes (left) and Avocado–Corn Salsa (right).

Mango Pesto Mojo

1/2 cup chopped fresh basil
1 1/2 teaspoons chopped garlic
1/4 cup chopped fresh spinach
1 tablespoon pine nuts, toasted
2 tablespoons olive oil
2 tablespoons red wine vinegar
1 tablespoon fresh lemon juice
2 tablespoons fresh lime juice
3/4 cup puréed mango
Salt and freshly ground pepper to taste

Avocado–Corn Salsa

1 cup fresh corn kernels, cooked
1 jalapeño chile, seeded and minced
2 tablespoons rice wine vinegar
1 tablespoon fresh lemon juice
1 tablespoon fresh lime juice
1 1/2 tablespoons olive oil
1/4 cup puréed papaya
1/2 tomato, diced
1/4 red onion, diced
1/4 sweet Texas onion, diced
1–2 Hass avocados (3/4 pound) in large chunks

Snapper

4 (6-ounce) red snapper fillets
2 tablespoons fresh lemon juice
Salt and freshly ground pepper to taste
1 tablespoon chopped fresh thyme
1/4 cup chopped pecans
1 tablespoon brown sugar
1 tablespoon olive oil

To make the **mango pesto mojo**, put all of the ingredients except the mango, salt, and pepper in a blender. Blend for 1 minute at low speed. Add the mango and pulse for a few seconds. Season with salt and pepper. Set aside.

To make the **avocado–corn salsa**, combine all of the ingredients except the avocados in a bowl. Blend well, then gently fold in the avocados.

Preheat the oven to 400°F. Place the snapper fillets on a baking sheet and rub them with the lemon juice, salt, pepper, and thyme. Gently press the pecans onto the top of each fillet, and then gently press the brown sugar onto the pecans.

In a large skillet, heat the olive oil over medium heat. Place the fillets in the skillet, pecan side down. Sauté for 30 to 40 seconds, then remove with a spatula and return to the baking sheet, pecan side up. Place in the oven and bake until opaque throughout, 5 to 8 minutes. Remove from the oven.

To serve, place a spoonful of the mojo on each plate and top with a snapper fillet. Place a spoonful of the salsa alongside. Serve immediately. Serves 4.

STRIPED BASS WITH CHILCOSTLE CHILE SAUCE

Robert Del Grande, Cafe Annie, Houston

Striped bass is a firm-fleshed fish with a skin that many people find especially delicious when cooked crisp. This delightful fish is very light and healthful. You can ask your fishmonger to fillet whole fish and give you the bones for homemade stock instead of using the store-bought indicated below. The color of the sauce will vary with the color of the chile.

4 striped sea bass fillets, skin on

Leek, Poblano, & Fennel Salad

2 cups fish stock, clam broth, or reconstituted fish bouillion

3 leeks (white part only), slit lengthwise, rinsed well, and sliced into quarter-size pieces

1 fennel bulb, tops discarded, cut into quarter-size pieces

1 poblano chile, charred, peeled, and diced into $1/4$-inch pieces

1 tablespoon butter

Salt to taste

Chilcostle Sauce (see recipe, page 136)

Garnish: fresh tarragon sprigs

To make the **salad**, bring the stock, broth or bouillion to a boil. Add the leeks and poach until tender, about 3 minutes. Scoop out the leeks with a slotted spoon or strainer and rinse under cold water. Reserve. Repeat the procedure with the fennel.

Melt the butter over medium heat in a skillet. Add the leeks, poblano, and fennel and sauté gently until heated through, a few minutes. Season lightly with salt.

In a nonstick skillet, sauté the bass fillets, skin side down, over high heat until the skin is crisp. Turn the fillets over. Reduce the heat and finish cooking the fish until the flesh is opaque throughout, about 5 minutes.

To serve, divide the leek mixture among 4 dinner plates and place a bass fillet on top of each one. Drizzle some **chilcostle sauce** around the fish and garnish with tarragon sprigs. Serve immediately. Serves 4.

SEA SCALLOPS AND GULF SHRIMP

Tim Keating, De Ville Restaurant, The Four Seasons Hotel, Houston

This dish of shellfish and vegetables defies the usual Texas reputation for large, high-cholesterol meals. Tender scallops are paired with shrimp, an important product of Texas. This recipe is time-consuming but worth the effort. Make porcini powder by processing dried porcini in a spice mill to a fine consistency.

Mushroom–Corn Nage

3/4 pound fresh white mushrooms, sliced
2 large leeks (white part only), slit lengthwise, rinsed well, and sliced
4 large shallots, sliced
1 elephant garlic clove, sliced, or 1 small garlic clove
1 tablespoon canola–olive oil blend
1 ounce dried shiitake mushrooms, broken into pieces
1 1/2 tablespoons chopped fresh parsley
Kernels cut from 1 ear of corn
About 4 cups canned vegetable consommé
Freshly ground pepper to taste

Scallops and Shrimp

12 medium-sized sea scallops
Freshly ground pepper to taste
Pinch of porcini powder
8 (21-25 count) Gulf shrimp, peeled and deveined
Salt to taste
Mist of canola or olive blended oils
4 portions of blanched and seasoned vegetables, including fresh corn kernels, roasted mushrooms, or others
Polenta (see recipe, page 130)

To make the **mushroom–corn nage**, place a medium-sized saucepan over medium heat. When it is hot, add the fresh mushrooms, leeks, shallots, garlic, and oil. Cook, moving the mixture constantly to keep it from sticking, until caramelized, 8 to 10 minutes. When a good color has been achieved, add the dried shiitakes, parsley, corn, and enough vegetable consommé to cover the mixture. Season with pepper and bring to a rolling boil. Reduce the heat to simmer and cook for 20 minutes. Remove from the heat and strain through a fine-mesh strainer. The broth will be a deep brown. Reduce the broth over medium heat until syrupy, about 10 minutes. Set aside.

To prepare **scallops**, season the scallops lightly with pepper and a little porcini powder. Mist a non-stick skillet with canola–olive oil blend and heat over medium-high heat. Add the scallops and sear on both sides until just browned. Remove from skillet and keep warm. Season the **shrimp** with salt and pepper and sauté in the same skillet, turning once, until cooked through and firm to the touch, about 2 minutes. Remove from the skillet and keep warm. Reheat the vegetables in boiling water.

To serve, place 3 triangles of **polenta** on each plate and top with 1 shrimp. Put 2 shrimp on top. Place the vegetables around the scallops and moisten with mushroom-corn nage. Serves 4.

CHICKEN MOLE

Moles are intense Mexican sauces containing herbs, chiles, chocolate, and seeds or nuts. Traditionally it's made by hand in a mortar, or molcajete, but many now make it in a blender. While there are as many types of moles as there are Mexicans, richly sauced chicken moles such as this one, are typical. Good accompaniments are Charro Beans (see recipe, page 127) made with pinto beans and sausage, Spanish Rice with tomatoes, garlic and herbs (see recipe, page 128), and Guacamole (see recipe, page 36).

Chicken Mole, served with Charro Beans (left), Spanish Rice (right), and Guacamole (center).

1 tablespoon olive oil plus 2 tablespoons
2 garlic cloves, minced
1 medium onion, chopped
2 tomatoes, peeled, seeded, and chopped
$1\frac{1}{2}$ teaspoons chopped almonds
$\frac{1}{2}$ teaspoon cinnamon
1 teaspoon cumin
$\frac{3}{4}$ teaspoon salt plus $\frac{1}{2}$ teaspoon
1 tablespoon raisins
2 dried chile peppers, seeded and chopped
$\frac{1}{2}$ cup chicken stock
$\frac{1}{2}$ teaspoon chile powder
1 ounce semisweet chocolate
1 chicken, quartered

Heat 1 tablespoon of the olive oil in a small skillet over medium heat. Add the garlic and onion and sauté for several minutes until tender. Transfer to a blender and add the tomatoes, almonds, cinnamon, cumin, $\frac{3}{4}$ teaspoon of the salt, raisins, dried chiles, chicken stock, and chile powder. Process until very smooth, about 10 minutes. Pour the mixture into a saucepan, add the chocolate, and cook over medium heat for 10 minutes to blend the flavors.

Preheat the oven to 350°F. Sprinkle the chicken quarters with the remaining $\frac{1}{2}$ teaspoon salt. In a skillet, heat the remaining 2 tablespoons olive oil over medium heat. Add the chicken quarters and brown well on all sides, but do not cook through. Place the browned chicken in a deep baking dish and cover with the mole sauce. Bake until the chicken meat pulls easily away from the bones, about 40 minutes. Serves 4; yields $2\frac{1}{3}$ cups sauce.

DUCK AND BLACK BEAN CASSOULET

Tim Keating, DeVille Restaurant, The Four Seasons Hotel, Houston

Here is an adaptation of the classic French dish of long-cooked beans, seasonings, and various meats. This variation uses black beans instead of the traditional white beans. Ideally, you need to start the cassoulet two days before you plan to serve it. Cheat if you must, however, as it's hard to spoil this dish. The duck legs confit, duck sausage, and duck fat can be ordered by mail.

Black Beans (see recipe, page 127)

Duck and Pork

1 pound duck legs, boned and cut into 1-inch cubes
1 pound pork shoulder, boned and cut into 1-inch cubes
Kosher salt and freshly ground pepper
6 tablespoons duck fat, divided
1 large onion, chopped
3 garlic cloves, diced
6 duck legs confit
6 ounces andouille sausage
¼ pound duck sausage
About 4 cups rich chicken stock
2 ripe plum tomatoes, peeled, seeded, and diced
1 *bouquet garni*, made with ½ bunch fresh thyme, 1 bay leaf, a few fresh parsley stems, and 8 peppercorns, wrapped in cheesecloth
2 poblano chiles, roasted, peeled, and diced
¾ cup corn bread crumbs

Season duck and pork cubes with salt and pepper. Sear duck in 2 tablespoons of duck fat over medium-high heat. Set aside. Repeat with pork.

In the same skillet, heat 2 tablespoons duck fat over medium heat. Add the onion and garlic and sauté until tender. Transfer to a large saucepan. In the same skillet, sear the duck legs and add to the pan. In the same skillet, brown the sausages and add to the pan. Deglaze the pan with a little chicken stock over high heat to dislodge the browned bits. Add to the pan along with tomatoes, bouquet garni, and chicken stock to cover. Cover and simmer until the meat is tender, about 1 hour. Add stock to keep the mixture a bit soupy. Adjust the seasonings, and simmer for 30 minutes. Remove the meat, sausages and bouquet garni. Cut the sausages into slices. Set aside.

Prepare the **black beans** then strain bean liquid and reduce by half. Pour half the beans into a large heatproof casserole or pot. Add cubed pork, duck, and chiles. Top with remaining beans, duck legs, and sausages. Cover with ¾ cup bean liquid. Cover and refrigerate. The next day, bring the casserole to room temperature. Sprinkle with ¼ cup bread crumbs and drizzle with 2 tablespoons of duck fat. Place in a roasting pan. Add hot water halfway up the sides of the casserole. Bake uncovered in a preheated 250°F oven until hot, about 1 hour. After 30 minutes, fold the crumbs down into the surface and top with ¼ cup of crumbs. After 10 minutes, fold in the crumbs again and top with remaining crumbs. Add bean liquid or stock if mixture becomes dry. To serve, brown the casserole under the broiler. Serve hot. Serves 6.

GRILLED TEXAS OSTRICH

Tim Keating, DeVille Restaurant, The Four Seasons Hotel, Houston

Ostrich farms are widespread across Texas. Ostriches are the largest birds in the world, and for over a hundred years Texas ranchers raised them specifically for their plumes; only later were they marketed as a very lean source of tasty meat. The biggest question was figuring out which muscle was tender and thus usable for steaks. After much research over many years, it has been decided that the best cuts lie in the fan fillet. Despite what many people say, ostrich meat does not look and taste like chicken. Indeed, properly cooked, ostrich fillets are closer to good Angus beef. Today, ostriches live on a diet of mostly grain instead of grass and get less exercise, which results in very lean meat. Ostrich, duck gizzard confit, and duck and veal stocks are available by mail order.

> Ostrich Mop (see recipe, page 135)
> Cabernet Glaze (see recipe, page 135)

Tian

> 8 eggplant slices, peeled and grilled
> 3 bell pepper halves, roasted, peeled, seeded, and quartered
> 4 lengthwise fennel slices, blanched for 2 minutes
> 8 carrot slices cut on the bias, blanched for 2 minutes
> 12 duck gizzards confit, sliced

Ostrich

> 4 (5-ounce) ostrich fan fillets
> 1 tablespoon olive oil
> Kosher salt and freshly ground pepper to taste
> 1/4 cup mop glaze

Garnish: 4 fresh Mexican marigold mint sprigs

To make the **tian**, prepare a grill, and preheat the oven to 375°F. Create vertical stacks with the vegetables, alternating with the sliced duck gizzards: begin with a slice of eggplant, then duck gizzard, fennel, duck, carrot slices, duck, pepper quarters, duck, then a second layer of eggplant. Place the stack in a shallow, well-oiled roasting pan. Roast in the oven until heated through, 8 to 10 minutes.

While the vegetable stacks are roasting, rub the **ostrich** steaks with the olive oil and season with salt and pepper. Place on the hot grill. Cook, turning once, for a few minutes on each side. As the steaks finish cooking, brush each one with the **mop** and continue to turn so they do not burn. Grill the ostrich as desired; medium-rare is recommended.

To serve, place a vegetable stack in the center of each serving plate. Top each with a cooked ostrich fillet. Drizzle with the glaze and garnish with the Mexican marigold mint sprigs. Serve immediately. Serves 4.

HONEY-FRIED CHICKEN

Stephen Pyles, Star Canyon, Dallas

Hot, crusty, fried chicken is on many people's list of favorite meals. A specialty from the deep south, it traveled west with settlers and became a staple Texas country food. Here it's served with spicy, mashed Sweet Potatoes (see recipe, page 133). Some include gravy made with the drippings from cooking the chicken. Fried chicken is also perfect to take on a picnic.

1 (3–3$\frac{1}{2}$ pounds) chicken
$\frac{1}{2}$ cup honey
2 tablespoons raspberry or other fruit vinegar
$\frac{1}{2}$ cup flour
2 tablespoons whole-wheat flour
2 teaspoons cayenne powder
2 eggs
$\frac{1}{4}$ cup buttermilk
1 cup vegetable oil
Salt and freshly ground pepper

Cut the chicken into 6 serving pieces, reserving the back-bone, neck and wings for stock. Stir the honey and vinegar together and pour over the chicken. Marinate at least 2 hours, stirring occasionally. In a bowl, combine flours and cayenne. Set aside. In another bowl, whisk together the eggs and buttermilk.

In a large skillet, heat the oil over medium-high heat to 300°F, cook at a low temperature to keep the honey from caramelizing too quickly and burning. Remove the chicken from the marinade and drain on paper towels. Dip the chicken in egg wash, season with salt and pepper, and dredge in the flour mixture, coating thoroughly. Strain the marinade and reserve 1 tablespoon for the sauce.

Gently drop the dark meat into the pan for 5 to 6 minutes on the first side until browned. Turn, add the white meat and continue cooking, adjusting the heat so the chicken browns evenly on both sides and is tender when pierced with a fork, 15 to 18 minutes for dark meat, and 10 to 12 minutes for white meat. Serve hot with mashed Sweet Potatoes (see recipe, page 133). Serves 4 to 6.

POMEGRANATE-MARINATED CHICKEN BREAST

Monica Pope, Boulevard Bistrot, Houston

Houston has an international population where many languages are spoken. This recipe, which combines the unique flavors of pomegranate molasses and Indian spices in the marinade with Texas-grown rice, is an example of the eclectic cuisine that exists in the state. Pomegranate molasses can be purchased in Middle Eastern food stores or by mail. You need to begin preparing this dish the day before you plan to serve it. Serve with seasonal vegetables, Spinach Raita (see recipe, page 133) and Texmati Rice (see recipe, page 129).

Spice Rub
- ¼ cup yellow mustard seeds
- ¼ cup cumin seeds
- ¼ cup fennel seeds
- 2 teaspoons peppercorns
- 2 teaspoons whole cloves
- 6 tablespoons fresh thyme leaves
- 5 teaspoons fresh rosemary

Pomegranate Molasses Marinade
- 2 tablespoons spice rub
- 1 tablespoon fresh lemon juice
- 3 tablespoons pomegranate molasses
- 4 tablespoons maple syrup
- 1 tablespoon minced garlic
- 1 tablespoon grated or crushed ginger root
- Kosher salt and freshly ground pepper to taste

- 6 boneless chicken breast halves

To make the **spice rub**, combine the mustard, cumin, fennel seeds, peppercorns, and cloves in a small skillet and toast over low heat until fragrant. Remove from the heat, let cool, and grind to a coarse powder in a spice mill. Transfer the spices to a mini processor, add the thyme and rosemary, and process until thoroughly blended. You will not need all of the spice rub for this dish. Measure out 2 tablespoons and transfer the remaining rub to an airtight container for another use.

To make the **marinade**, combine the spice rub, lemon juice, 1 tablespoon of the pomegranate molasses, 2 tablespoons of the maple syrup, the garlic, ginger, salt, and pepper in a small bowl. Rub the marinade on both sides of the chicken breasts and place in a shallow dish. Cover and marinate for at least 4 hours in the refrigerator. Combine the remaining 2 tablespoons each pomegranate molasses and maple syrup and set aside.

Preheat the oven to 350°F. Place a sauté pan over medium high heat, add the chicken, and sear on both sides until nicely browned, 1 to 2 minutes. Transfer to an ovenproof pan. Pour the reserved pomegranate and maple syrup over the chicken, transfer to the oven, and cook until the juices run clear, about 30 to 35 minutes. Serves 6.

ROASTED BABY CHICKEN

Scott Cohen, Las Canarias, La Mansion del Rio, San Antonio

Pousin and Cornish hens are small chickens that weigh about a pound with the bones, half that if boneless. In this case they are boneless except for the leg, and your butcher can do the work for you. They are cooked in individual small skillets and make a unique presentation when served from them directly from the oven to the table. Or, choose an attractive platter and serve the stuffing alongside with stewed okra and tomatoes (page 131), a favorite farm dish.

Cornbread Stuffing
1/2 **pound cornbread (may be purchased)**
1 1/2 **teaspoons butter**
1/4 **cup diced celery**
1/4 **cup diced carrots**
1/4 **cup diced wild mushrooms**
2 **tablespoons chopped fresh sage**
Salt and freshly ground pepper to taste
1/2 **cup (or more) chicken stock**

4 **(1-pound) baby chickens, boned**

Glaze
1/4 **cup chicken stock**
1/2 **cup demi-glace**

To make the **stuffing**, preheat the oven to 350°F. Dice the cornbread and put in a mixing bowl. In a skillet over medium heat, melt the butter and add the celery and carrots. Reduce the heat to low and cook slowly until the vegetables are translucent and tender. Add the mushrooms and continue to sweat the vegetables without browning. Add the vegetables to the cornbread and gently mix in the sage, and salt and pepper to taste. Transfer to a buttered baking dish. Pour the chicken stock over the stuffing and bake for one-half hour. Remove from the oven and set aside to cool.

Make the **glaze** by heating the chicken stock and the demi-glace in a small saucepan. Set aside half to serve as sauce.

Preheat the oven to 450°F. When the cornbread stuffing has cooled, put about 3/4 cup into the cavity of each chicken. Transfer the chickens to the rack of a baking pan and roast 20 minutes or until golden brown. While the chicken is roasting, brush from time to time with the glaze.

To serve, remove the stuffing from the chickens and serve at the side with the sauce. Serves 4.

HARISSA DUCK

Monica Pope, Boulevard Bistrot, Houston

Hunting is a big sport in the state, and there are many hunt clubs that arrange trips, private landowners who lease their property to hunting enthusiasts, and organizations that take tour groups duck hunting. There is a lot of flavor in the duck skin, but it is very fatty. Leaving it on is optional. Serve with fiery harissa sauce, carrot pudding, and seasonal vegetables.

Harissa Sauce

10 garlic cloves, chopped
3 tablespoons paprika
$1\frac{1}{3}$ tablespoons caraway seeds
$1\frac{1}{2}$–$2\frac{1}{2}$ tablespoons cayenne pepper
$1\frac{1}{2}$–$2\frac{1}{2}$ tablespoons crushed red pepper flakes
$2\frac{1}{2}$ teaspoons ground coriander
$1\frac{1}{4}$ teaspoons ground cumin
$1\frac{1}{4}$ teaspoons kosher salt
$1\frac{1}{4}$ teaspoons extra-virgin olive oil
$\frac{3}{4}$ teaspoon ground aniseed
$\frac{1}{2}$ cup plus 2 tablespoons fresh lime juice

8 boneless duck breast halves

Indian Carrot Pudding

6 cups milk
8 green cardamom pods, split open
$2\frac{1}{2}$ pounds carrots, grated
$\frac{1}{2}$–$\frac{2}{3}$ cup sugar
2 tablespoons clarified butter
1 tablespoon slivered almonds
2 tablespoons golden raisins
$\frac{1}{4}$ teaspoon ground cardamom
$\frac{1}{2}$ cup heavy cream, lightly whipped

Harissa Duck, served here with cauliflower, Carrot Pudding, and extra Harissa sauce.

To make **harissa sauce**, combine all of the ingredients in a bowl and mix well. Measure out $\frac{1}{4}$ cup and reserve. Put the duck breasts in a shallow dish and pour the rest of the harissa sauce over, to coat thoroughly. Cover and marinate for at least 2 hours.

To make the **carrot pudding**, combine the milk and cardamom pods in a saucepan and bring to a boil while stirring. Reduce the heat to medium and boil slowly until reduced by half, 15 to 20 minutes. Remove the cardamom pods. Add the carrots and cook for another 35 to 45 minutes, stirring occasionally. Once all of the liquid has cooked away, add $\frac{1}{2}$ cup of the sugar or more, mixing well. Remove the pan from the heat. In a small skillet, heat the clarified butter and add the almonds. As they start to brown, add the raisins and sauté until they plump. Remove from the heat and add the ground cardamom. Immediately pour the mixture into the carrots and mix well. Fold in the lightly whipped cream. Keep warm.

Preheat the oven to between 350° and 375° F. In a large ovenproof sauté pan or skillet, sear the duck on both sides over medium high heat, then transfer to the oven. Cook until fork-tender and the juices run clear, about 10 minutes.

Serve with the remaining fiery hot harissa sauce on the side. Serves 6 to 8.

GRILLED QUAIL WITH PECAN COUSCOUS

Scott Cohen, Las Canarias, La Mansion del Rio, San Antonio

Quail has always been a favorite game bird for frying and smothering in gravy. But, these days you're just as likely to find it in an elegant setting like this—grilled and resting in a pool of lemon hazelnut sauce, nestled between toasted pecan couscous and a citrus salad with an apple cider vinaigrette, resulting in a burst of flavors. You'll find quail almost everywhere—in the supermarket, at the butcher, even by mail order. This isn't a quick recipe, but the sauces aren't difficult and can be made in advance. Have your butcher bone the quail for you. This recipe is also great as an appetizer. Simply cut the proportions by half. Serve with Citrus Salad with Apple Cider Vinaigrette (see recipe, page 134).

Lemon Hazelnut Sauce
  2 (4-ounce) sticks of butter
  Juice of 2 lemons
  4 tablespoons demi glace (store-bought)
  4 tablespoons hazelnut oil
  2 tablespoons chopped chives
  Salt
  2 teaspoons crushed peppercorns

Couscous
  1 cup plain packaged couscous
  1½ cups chicken broth
  4 tablespoons chopped rosemary
  1 cup pecans, toasted and chopped
  Salt and freshly ground pepper

Quail
  8 quail, boned except for the legs and wings,
    cut down the back to open flat

To make the **sauce**, brown the butter in a small saucepan over moderate heat, being careful not to burn it. Add the remaining ingredients and stir until well blended. Keep warm.

To make the **couscous**, cook the couscous according to package directions, substituting chicken broth for water and adding the rosemary. After 5 minutes, stir in the toasted pecans. Season with salt and pepper. Keep warm.

To make the **quail**, cook the quail on a grill or in a sauté pan over moderate heat, 2 to 4 minutes per side for medium. Serve two quail per person on top of a little lemon hazelnut sauce. Divide the couscous and citrus salad among the plates. Serves 4.

BEEF FAJITAS WITH NOPALES

Fajitas used to refer to grilled skirt steak, but now it's popular to make them with not only beef, but also chicken or shrimp. The meat or seafood is marinated, grilled, sliced, and rolled in tortillas with fillings like peppers, onions, and garnishes. Sautéed cactus paddles, or nopales, is a unique specialty.

Fajitas

2 cups light soy sauce
1 cup firmly packed dark brown sugar
$1/4$ teaspoon ground cumin
2 garlic cloves, minced
1 onion, coarsely chopped
$1/2$ teaspoon cayenne pepper
$1/4$ cup fresh lemon juice
$1^{1}/_{2}$ tablespoons chopped ginger root
$1^{1}/_{2}$ pounds skirt steak
1 green bell pepper, cut into $1/4$-inch strips
1 onion, cut into $1/2$-inch-wide strips

6 (8-inch) flour tortillas, warmed

Nopales

2 cups cubed cactus paddle, "eyes" removed
Pinch of baking soda
1 tablespoon canola oil
$1/2$ cup thinly sliced onion
2 garlic cloves, minced
$1/2$ jalapeño chile, minced, or to taste
1 large tomato, seeded and chopped
Fresh lime juice to taste
Salt and freshly ground pepper to taste
2 tablespoons chopped fresh cilantro

Combine the ingredients except the steak, pepper, and onion strips. Refrigerate several hours.

Remove $1/2$ cup of marinade and reserve. Put the steak into the remaining marinade, and refrigerate for 3–4 hours. When the beef has marinated, toss the peppers and onions in the reserved marinade.

Cook the steak on a hot grill for 4 minutes per side. Remove the pepper and onion from the marinade and sauté over medium heat until tender. Remove the steak from the grill and slice across the grain into $1/4$-inch slices. Place the beef, peppers, and onions on tortillas. Garnish with shredded Monterey Jack cheese, Fresh Tomato Salsa (see recipe, page 36), Guacamole (page 36), and sour cream.

In water to cover, bring the cactus and baking soda to a boil. Reduce heat, simmer until tender. Drain and rinse well in warm water to reduce the slippery consistency. Dry on paper towels. In a skillet, heat the oil over medium heat. Sauté onions, garlic, and jalapeño until translucent. Add the tomato and cook until it breaks down. Add the lime juice and nopales. Season and add the cilantro. Serve warm. Serves 4 to 6.

COWBOY RIB-EYE STEAK

Stephan Pyles, Star Canyon, Dallas

If you ask a Texan, you'll hear that their state has the best beef in the world. The rib-eye is a prime example of what they're bragging about. It is a cut of meat from the rib, with a lot of marbling that contributes to the fine flavor. These large portions weigh about a pound each. Adjust the size according to your appetite. The cowboy rub can be made ahead of time and stored.

4 bone-in rib-eye steaks, 14 to 16 ounces each
Cowboy Rub (see recipe, page 135)

$1/2$ cup dried pinto beans, soaked overnight and drained
1 quart ham hock broth or water
Salt and freshly ground pepper to taste
1 tablespoon clarified butter or vegetable oil
2 tablespoons minced shallots
2 garlic cloves, minced
$1^1/2$ cups assorted fresh wild mushrooms, cleaned and sliced (such as morels, chanterelles, oysters or shiitakes)
$1^1/2$ cups fresh corn kernels
$1/2$ cup dry red wine
$1^1/2$ cups veal demiglace
1 teaspoon chipotle chile purée
1 teaspoon chopped sage
1 medium tomato, blanched, peeled, seeded and diced
1 tablespoon chopped basil
1 tablespoon unsalted butter, at room temperature

Onion Rings (see recipe, page 133)
***Garnish:* $1/2$ cup pico de gallo (see page 44)**

Place the beans in a saucepan with the broth or water. Bring to a boil, reduce the heat to a simmer and cook for 45 minutes to 1 hour checking every 20 minutes or so. Add more broth or water as needed to keep the beans covered. Once tender, season and reserve.

Heat the clarified butter or oil in a large skillet or pan over medium heat until lightly smoking. Add the shallots and garlic and cook for 20 seconds. Add the mushrooms and corn, and cook for 1 minute longer. Deglaze the pan with the red wine and reduce the liquid by three-quarters over high heat. Add the demiglace, chipotle purée, sage, reserved beans, and tomato. Reduce the liquid by one-third, add the basil, whisk in the butter, and season with salt. Keep the sauce warm.

To prepare the **steaks,** coat each side of the steaks with the **Cowboy Rub**. Let stand for at least one hour. Prepare a medium-hot grill and cook the steaks until the exterior is very brown and crusty, about 7 to 8 minutes per side. If flare-ups occur on the grill, remove the steak from the grill using long tongs, wait for the fire to calm, then place the steak back on the grill. Remove the steaks from the fire and allow them to rest for 5 minutes before serving.

To serve, ladle the sauce generously onto plates. Add steak, and top with **onion rings**. Garnish with pico de gallo. Serves 4.

FILLET OF BEEF ROASTED WITH COFFEE BEANS

Robert Del Grande, Cafe Annie, Houston

A coating of coffee and cocoa and a chile broth take fillet of beef to new heights in this contemporary preparation. Grits with bitter greens and mushrooms are a nod to the pantry of the South. Spinach is a good alternative to the bitter greens.

1 (2-pound) fillet of beef, preferably cut from the large end of the whole fillet
1 teaspoon coarse salt
1 teaspoon freshly ground pepper
2 tablespoons extra-virgin olive oil
2 tablespoons very finely ground coffee beans
1 tablespoon cocoa powder
$1/8$ teaspoon ground cinnamon

Creamy White Grits (see recipe, page 129)

$3/4$ pound fresh shiitake mushrooms, stems removed and caps cut into quarters
2 tablespoons butter
$1/2$ yellow onion, minced
2 garlic cloves, minced

$1/4$ pound arugula or other bitter green, coarsely chopped
Pasilla Chile Broth (see recipe, page 136)
Garnish: Watercress sprigs

Tie the fillet of beef with kitchen string at $1/2$-inch intervals. Sprinkle the fillet with the salt and pepper and rub it with the olive oil. Combine the ground coffee, cocoa powder, and cinnamon in a small bowl and mix well. Spread the mixture over a work surface and roll the fillet in the mixture to coat evenly. Let stand for about 30 minutes.

Preheat the oven to 400°F. Place the fillet on the rack in a roasting pan and roast for 10 minutes. Immediately reduce the heat to 250°F. After 20 minutes check the internal temperature of the fillet. It should be 125°F for medium-rare or 135°F for medium. If further cooking is necessary, return the beef to the oven and slowly roast to the desired temperature. Remove from the oven and keep warm.

Melt 1 tablespoon butter in a skillet over medium-high heat until foaming. Add the mushrooms and sauté for a few minutes until translucent. Set aside. Keep warm.

To finish the **grits**, put 1 tablespoon of butter in a different skillet. Sauté the onion and garlic until translucent. Stir in the greens and sauté until wilted. Add the vegetable mixture to the cooked grits.

Remove the string from the fillet and slice into $1/4$-inch-thick slices. Spoon some of the grits and some of the mushrooms onto each plate. Arrange the slices of the fillet around the grits. Ladle some of the **pasilla broth** over the fillet slices. Garnish with watercress sprigs. Serves 4 to 6.

MOROCCAN BRAISED LAMB SHANKS

Monica Pope, Boulevard Bistrot, Houston

Lamb shanks are delicious when rubbed with this intense curry mixture, marinated overnight, then braised for several hours, making the lamb fall-off-the-bone tender.

Curry Mixture

2 tablespoons plus 2 teaspoons ground cumin
2 tablespoons plus 2 teaspoons ground coriander
2 tablespoons plus 2 teaspoons mustard seeds
4 teaspoons fennel seeds
4 teaspoons ground cloves
2 teaspoons dill seeds
$2^{1}/_{2}$ sticks cinnamon, crushed
4 teaspoons black peppercorns
4 teaspoons cayenne pepper
2 tablespoons plus 2 teaspoons turmeric

6 lamb shanks
All-purpose flour for coating
Salt and freshly ground pepper to taste
2 tablespoons olive oil
About 4 quarts chicken or veal stock
2–3 sprigs fresh mint, chopped

Lamb Braising Liquid (see recipe, page 136)
Lentils with Dried Apricots (see recipe, page 134)

The day before serving, make the **curry mixture**. Combine all the ingredients except the red pepper and turmeric in a dry pan over medium heat and toast until fragrant. Transfer the toasted spices to a spice grinder and grind to a powder. Empty the spices into a bowl and stir in the red pepper and turmeric. Rub the curry mixture onto each shank, coating well, cover, and refrigerate overnight.

The next day, on a large plate, mix together the flour, salt, and pepper. Dust each shank lightly with the flour mixture, shaking off the excess. In a skillet, sear the shanks on all sides in olive oil over medium-high heat to seal in the juices before braising. Do not cook through. Set aside.

Preheat the oven to 350°F. Put the lamb shanks in an ovenproof pan big enough to hold them and the **braising liquid**. Add the braising liquid and up to 4 quarts stock, or as needed to cover the shanks. Cover with aluminum foil and place in the oven. Cook until tender when pierced with a knife, $2^{1}/_{2}$ to $3^{1}/_{2}$ hours.

Remove the shanks from the braising liquid and keep warm. Add the fresh mint to 6 cups of the braising liquid and reduce in a sauté pan to 3 cups.

To serve, place about $^{3}/_{4}$ cup of the **lentils** on each plate. Place a shank on top and pour the reduced mint-infused braising liquid over the top. Serves 6.

PORK LOIN WITH COCOA CHILE PASTE

Robert Del Grande, Cafe Annie, Houston

There's nothing pedestrian about pork when it is cooked in this elegant way: pork loin rubbed with a deeply flavored seasoning paste, roasted, and served with a fabulous barbecue sauce.

Seasoning Paste

- $\frac{1}{4}$ cup cocoa powder
- 1 tablespoon ancho chile powder
- 1 tablespoon ground cinnamon
- 1 tablespoon brown sugar
- 1 teaspoon coarse salt
- $\frac{1}{2}$ teaspoon freshly ground pepper
- $\frac{1}{4}$ cup olive oil
- 1 teaspoon balsamic vinegar

- 2 ($\frac{1}{2}$ pound) pork loins, placed side by side and tied together at 1-inch intervals

Drip Pan BBQ Sauce

- 4 plum tomatoes, quartered
- 4 (about 1 ounce) pasilla chiles, stems removed and seeded
- 1 chipotle chile in adobo sauce
- 1 tablespoon adobo sauce from canned chipotles
- 6 prunes, chopped
- $\frac{1}{2}$ white onion, chopped
- 4 garlic cloves, chopped
- 1 cup firmly packed brown sugar
- $1\frac{1}{2}$ cups white vinegar
- $1\frac{1}{2}$ teaspoons coarse salt

Preheat the oven to 425°F. To make the **seasoning paste**, combine well the ingredients in a small bowl to form a paste. Brush the pork loin with the paste.

Place the loin on a rack in a large roasting pan and place in the oven. After 5 minutes, reduce the heat to 250°F. Over the next $1\frac{1}{2}$ hours, the temperature of the oven will slowly decline. Do not open the oven door during this time. After $1\frac{1}{2}$ hours, check the internal temperature of the pork roast. If it is not between 155 and 160°F, continue to roast the pork loin at 250°F for another 20 minutes or until the pork reaches the desired temperature.

While the pork loin is roasting, prepare the **BBQ sauce**: combine all of the ingredients for the sauce in a saucepan along with 2 cups water. Bring to a boil, reduce the heat, cover partially, and simmer, stirring occasionally, for about 30 minutes. Remove from the heat and set aside to cool. Transfer the sauce to a blender and purée until smooth. If the consistency is too thick, thin it with a little water.

Remove the pork roast from the oven, remove from the pan, and set aside to cool. Add $\frac{1}{2}$ cup water to the roasting pan, scrape any browned bits from the pan bottom, then add the contents of the pan to the puréed sauce.

To serve, carve the pork loin into thin slices. Serve the BBQ sauce on the side. Serves 8.

ANTELOPE WITH HONEY-MALT GLAZE

Dean Fearing, The Mansion on Turtle Creek, Dallas

This innovative recipe showcases antelope, which is commercially raised in Texas. It is cooked like venison, but since it isn't as lean, it doesn't require as much basting. The tomato-pozole stew can be served as an independent dish, and, of course, fajitas are a typical Texas snack food that are served anytime, any place. Antelope can be ordered by mail.

Honey-Malt Glaze
$3/4$ teaspoon canola oil
1 red bell pepper, seeded and chopped
$1/2$ small onion, chopped
1 garlic clove, minced
$1^1/2$ teaspoons annatto seeds
$1/2$ cup honey
$1/4$ cup malt vinegar
Salt and freshly ground pepper to taste

Antelope
4 (6-ounce) antelope tenderloin fillets, trimmed of all fat and silver skin
Salt and freshly ground pepper to taste
1 tablespoon canola oil

Yellow Tomato–Pozole Stew
  (see recipe, page 132)
Barbecued Venison Fajitas
  (see recipe, page 133)
Garnish: 4 fresh cilantro sprigs

An antelope fillet sits on a bed of Yellow Tomato–Pozole Stew, paired with a Barbecued Venison Fajita (rear).

To make the **glaze**, heat the oil in a medium-size saucepan over medium-high heat. Add the bell peppers, onion, garlic, and annatto seeds and sauté until the onion is translucent, about 2 minutes. Add the honey and cook until reduced by one-third, about 2 minutes. Add the malt vinegar and reduce by one-third, about 1 minute. Allow to cool. Pour the mixture into a blender and puree until smooth. Season with salt and pepper. Reserve.

Season the antelope with salt and pepper. In a large skillet or sauté pan, heat the canola oil over medium-high heat. Add as many fillets as will fit in a single layer without crowding. Cook, turning once, for 2 minutes on each side, to medium-rare. Repeat as needed to sauté all the fillets. About 1 minute before the fillets have finished cooking, brush on a generous amount of honey-malt glaze. Turn each fillet and cook until the glaze thickens, about 1 minute. Remove from the pan and keep warm until serving.

Place a portion of **pozole stew** on 4 warmed dinner plates. Place an antelope fillet on top of each portion of the stew, and place a **venison fajita** next to the fillet. Garnish with a cilantro sprig. Serve immediately. Serves 4.

CHICKEN-FRIED VENISON STEAKS

Grady Spears, Reata Restaurants, Alpine/Fort Worth

Early German settlers in Texas are given credit for adapting Wiener schnitzel recipes from their homeland into the now-famous chicken-fried steak. Popular in the South and the Midwest, it's a Texas specialty, and reports put the state's daily consumption at more than 800,000 steaks. Typically, a less tender cut of beef like round steak is used, but here venison is tenderized, floured, and fried crisp like chicken and served with a thick milk gravy. Serve with mashed potatoes and green beans with red onion, red bell pepper strips and bacon bits.

Pepper and onion-studded green beans and thick mashed potatoes make a great accompaniment to Chicken Fried Venison Steaks.

Spiced Flour

1¼ cups all-purpose flour
3 tablespoons kosher salt
3 tablespoons freshly ground pepper
2 tablespoons sugar

Venison

3 eggs
⅓ cup buttermilk
½ cup beer, preferably Lone Star
6 (10-ounce) tenderized venison cutlets
2 cups peanut oil

Gravy

⅓ cup unsalted butter
6 tablespoons all-purpose flour
2 ½ cups milk
2 teaspoons kosher salt
2 teaspoons minced fresh sage
2 teaspoons Tabasco or other hot-pepper sauce

To make the **spiced flour**, combine all the ingredients in a shallow dish and mix well.

To make the **venison**, whisk together the eggs, buttermilk, and beer in a bowl. Dredge a venison cutlet in the spiced flour, coating well. Place the floured venison in the egg mixture, again coating well. Dredge the venison again through the spiced flour. Repeat this process with the remaining cutlets.

Pour the peanut oil into a deep pan and heat to 375°F. In batches, place the breaded cutlets in the hot oil and cook, turning once, until crusty brown, 3 to 4 minutes on each side. Transfer to paper towels or a rack to drain. Keep warm.

To make the **gravy**, melt the butter in a saucepan over medium heat. Whisk in the flour, stirring constantly until well blended and there are no lumps. Add the milk, a little at a time, whisking to keep the gravy smooth. Season with salt, sage, and Tabasco and continue to simmer about 5 minutes, or until the gravy. Serve the venison steaks with the gravy. Serves 6.

GRILLED RIB-EYE STEAK

Today, three-quarters of American households have a grill, and the variety of grills available on the market increases as quickly as the popularity of cooking outdoors. Besides taking the cooking out of the kitchen, cooking food on an outdoor grill delivers unbeatable flavor. For this cookout, the rib-eye steaks are a little smaller than the one-pounders (or more) you often see on steakhouse menus. They are well marbled, and along with the porterhouse and the T-bone, are one of the best beef cuts you'll find. They only need a few turns of the pepper grinder and a few minutes over a hot grill. Top the cooked steaks with a slice of cilantro butter. Alongside, serve Confetti Corn studded with red and green bell peppers (see recipe, page 130) and fresh tender stalks of asparagus wrapped in bacon.

Cilantro Butter

1/4 cup (1/2 stick) unsalted butter, at room
    temperature
6 tablespoons chopped fresh cilantro
3/4 teaspoon ground cumin
1/4 teaspoon chile powder
1 teaspoon salt

4 (10-ounce) rib-eye steaks, trimmed of
    excess fat
Freshly ground pepper

To prepare the **cilantro butter**, combine all of the ingredients in a food processor and pulse until the butter is light and creamy and the cilantro is finely chopped. Scoop the butter out onto a piece of plastic wrap and shape it into a log 1 1/2 inches in diameter. Wrap in the plastic wrap and refrigerate well. When chilled, cut into slices.

Prepare a hot fire in a grill. Season each **steak** with pepper and place on the grill. Cook, turning once, for 4 to 5 minutes on each side for medium-rare.

Remove the steaks from the grill and place on dinner plates. Immediately put a slice of cilantro butter on the top of each steak. Serves 4.

SMOKED BRISKET

The brisket is a slightly triangular-shaped cut of beef from the underside forequarter of the cow and is very fibrous with a lot of connective tissue. Since it is tough, barbecuing will break down the collagen and tenderize it. In the days of chuck wagon cooking, brisket was a popular range meal because it cooked for a long time and fed a lot of cowhands. Smoked brisket cooked slowly over a low temperature will be moist and tender. Good side dishes are Tex-Mex Cornbread (see recipe, page 129), Outlaw Cole Slaw (page 131), Roasted Corn on the Cob with Jalapeño-Lime Butter (page 131), and Pickled Okra (page 36).

A feast of smoked brisket goes well with (from left to right): Outlaw Coleslaw, Tex-Mex Cornbread, Texas Caviar, and Pickled Okra.

1 (5–8 pound) brisket, untrimmed

Dry Rub

$\frac{1}{4}$ **cup paprika**
$\frac{1}{4}$ **cup salt**
2 tablespoons black pepper
2 tablespoons garlic powder
2 tablespoons ground cumin
2 tablespoons brown sugar
1 tablespoon chile powder
1 tablespoon cayenne pepper
1 teaspoon dried oregano
1 teaspoon dry mustard

Hardwood charcoal briquettes
Hardwood chunks or chips, soaked at least
    30 minutes in water, beer, or wine
Water pan (optional)
Tumbleweed BBQ Sauce (see recipe, page 134)

The day before you smoke the brisket, trim all but a $\frac{1}{2}$-inch layer of fat from the fat side of the brisket. Combine the dry rub ingredients thoroughly and rub it in well on both sides of the meat. Place the brisket in an airtight bag and refrigerate overnight.

Remove beef and let it come to room temperature. Prepare a smoker, and when the fire has settled to between 200 and 225°F, place a handful of soaked wood chunks onto the coals. Put the meat in the smoking chamber, fatty side up and close the top. For a grill, build the fire on one side and fill a water pan with water or beer and put it under the rack in the middle of the cooker. Place the brisket on the grill, fatty side up, on the opposite side of the fire and over the water pan if possible. Close the lid.

Cook the brisket for about 2 hours, then scatter another handful of soaked wood onto the fire or coals. By adjusting the air vents keep the temperature at about 225°F for 4 hours, then reduce heat to between 180 and 200°F. If you're not using a water pan, use tongs and remove the brisket from the grill after 3 to 4 hours and wrap it tightly in foil and put it back in the smoker. Total cooking time will be 5 to 6 hours, or even up to 10 hours. The internal temperature of the brisket should be between 165 and 170°F. Remove and let stand 15 to 20 minutes before carving. Cut away the fat and trim.

When ready to serve, place the brisket on a cutting board and carve across the grain in $\frac{1}{4}$-inch slices. Serve with **BBQ sauce** on the side. Serves 8 to 10.

T-BONE STEAK WITH SKILLET POTATOES

Michael Velardi, Pappas Brothers Steakhouse, Houston

Judging cuts of beef can be tricky business, but there's no doubt that porterhouse is the superior steak, the prized cut of beef. Technically, it comes from the short loin section of the cow where the tenderloin is the thickest, and includes the strip sirloin. Only two or three porterhouse steaks can be cut from the short loin of beef. The short loin can, however, be cut into T-bone steaks, which are the same as the porterhouse but contain less of the filet mignon, and also into club and shell steaks (which contain none of the filet mignon). T-bones are a popular cut of steak typically served with a side of skillet potatoes.

3 pounds potatoes, unpeeled
2 tablespoons olive oil
1 onion, in ¼-inch slices
Pinch of sugar
3 strips thick smoky bacon
1 tablespoon bacon drippings
2 tablespoons butter
Pinch of salt, coarsely ground pepper,
  and sugar
2 teaspoons chopped garlic
2 tablespoons thinly sliced scallions

4 (25–30 ounce) T-bone steaks
Salt and coarsely black pepper

Cook the potatoes in boiling water. Drain then refrigerate the potatoes for about 2 hours or until cool. Peel and slice ¼-to ½-inch thick.

Heat the oil in a small skillet over medium heat and add the onions. Stir constantly as the onions sizzle and begin to brown. Add a pinch of salt, pepper, and sugar and cook until brown and caramelized. Remove from the heat and set aside.

In a cast-iron skillet, cook the bacon until crisp. Remove and drain on absorbent paper. When cool, crumble the bacon and set aside. Drain the bacon drippings from the pan except for 1 tablespoon. In the same pan, add the butter to the bacon drippings. Add the sliced potatoes, season with salt and pepper, and cook over medium heat until the bottom is crisp. Turn the potatoes over and season the other side with salt and pepper. Add the garlic, caramelized onions, scallions, and crumbled bacon. Cook until they are tender then keep warm while cooking the steak.

Prepare a hot grill. Season the steaks with salt and pepper and cook for approximately 8 to 10 minutes per side for medium-rare, or as desired. Remove from the grill and top with a spoonful of parsley butter. Serve with skillet potatoes. Serves 4.

SPICED VEAL CHOP

Danielle Custer, Laurels Restaurant, Westin Park Central Hotel, Dallas

Veal is young beef, less than a year old, with fine-textured meat that contains very little fat. It is delicately flavored and corresponds to the section of beef from where the porterhouse, T-bone and sirloin steaks are cut. This preparation blends African and Latin flavors by using a spice rub for the veal, with a pepian, a classic green mole sauce primarily made of chiles and a binder such as bread or nuts. It's accompanied by matoke mash, a plantain mixture eaten in Africa and garnished with fried plantains.

Spice Rub
1/2 teaspoon black peppercorns
1/2 teaspoon celery seeds
1/4 teaspoon cayenne pepper
1/2 teaspoon dried thyme
2 teaspoons paprika
2 teaspoons dry mustard, preferably Coleman's
1/2 teaspoon salt
2 teaspoons brown sugar

Veal
4 (14-ounce) veal chops
Salt and freshly ground pepper

Pepian (see recipe, page 137)
Matoke Mash (see recipe, page 137)
Banana Mojo (see recipe, page 137)

Garnish (optional)
1 medium green plantain
3 1/2 cups peanut oil
Salt

To make the **spice rub**, grind the peppercorns and celery seeds separately in a spice mill. Combine with the remaining ingredients and store in an airtight container.

To cook the **veal**, prepare a medium hot grill. Season the veal with salt and pepper. Rub the meat on both sides with spice rub. Sear the chops on one side for 3 1/2 minutes, rotate the meat 45 degrees to make grill marks. Continue to grill for 3 1/2 minutes. Turn the veal over and repeat on the other side, for a total cooking time of 14 minutes for medium. Remove from the grill and let rest for 10 minutes before serving.

To make the **plantains**, slice them very thinly, lengthwise, using a mandoline. Heat the oil to 375° F in a deep fry pan. Cook a few at a time until lightly browned, 2 1/2 to 3 minutes. Drain on paper toweling and season with salt.

To serve, spoon some of the warm **Pepian** onto the plate. Place some **Metoke Mash** in the center of each plate and rest the veal against it. Spoon some dollops of **Banana Mojo** on top of the pepian sauce and garnish with the fried plantains. Serves 4.

SPARERIBS AND ALL THE FIXIN'S

Although Texas is primarily a beef state, and giant beef ribs are still a mainstay in many areas, pork ribs have gradually taken the lead in popularity as a barbecue favorite. Like all ribs, they should be cooked slowly, over low temperature, and enhanced with rich smokiness from wood. Ribs are purchased in slabs (at least 11 bones) or racks (half a slab), and you can count on about 1 pound of ribs per person. Fixin's include German Bacon-laced Potato Salad (page 131), Bunkhouse Baked Beans (page 128), Cat Head Biscuits (page 129), and ice-cold watermelon—all of which can be rustled up the day before. Like other barbecue controversies, there are dry-rib fans who prefer theirs without barbecue sauce, and wet-rib fans who can't imagine eating a rib without spicy sauce. For more confusion, some folks are definitive about the value of marinating the ribs before cooking. This method is for dry-rib fans who like a spicy crust finish.

2 (3-pound) slabs meaty pork spare ribs, trimmed

Spicy Rib Rub
½ cup brown sugar
½ cup chile powder
½ cup granulated garlic
2 tablespoons paprika
2 tablespoons black pepper
1 tablespoon ground cumin
1 tablespoon dry mustard
Vegetable oil

Hard wood chips, soaked at least 30 minutes in water, beer, wine, or juice

Remove the membrane from the ribs by laying them on the counter, meat side down. With a knife or screwdriver, lift up and peel the membrane from the bone, starting at the end.

Combine the rib rub ingredients with just enough oil to slightly moisten the mixture so it will adhere to the ribs. Rub the seasoning liberally on both sides of the ribs. Place in a plastic bag or covered container in one layer and refrigerate for 2 hours, preferably overnight.

Heat an indirect fire in a charcoal grill or smoker to a temperature of 200°F. Add a handful of woodchips to the coals in the firebox. When the heat seems stable, place the ribs on the grill, bone side down, as far from the fire as possible. Barbecue at 200 to 235°F for 3½ to 4½ hours, the longer, the more tender they will be. Add more chips to the firebox as needed. If the ribs seem dry, baste with beer or wine. Test the ribs by pinching or tearing a little of the meat from the bones. It should pull away easily when done. The internal temperature of the meat at the thick end of the slab should be between 155° and 160°F. They should be crisp on the outside, juicy inside.

When done, remove the ribs and let them cool for about 10 minutes. To serve, cut the ribs bone side up into 3- or 4-bone segments. Serves 6.

RACK OF VENISON WITH SWEET POTATO GRATIN

Scott Cohen, Las Canarias, La Mansion del Rio, San Antonio

A rack of venison is cooked similar to a rack of lamb. This preparation is the most obvious example of a simple, well-conceived dish, showcasing the leanness and flavor of venison, it needs no adornment other than salt and pepper. Sweet potatoes, black fig demi-glace and red cabbage make good side dishes.

Black Fig Demi-glace
   1 pint (canned) veal or duck demi-glace
   6 dried black figs, thinly sliced

Sweet Potatoes
   3 medium sweet potatoes, cooked
   1 cup heavy cream
   1 tablespoon butter
   Salt and freshly ground white pepper
   Allspice, to taste
   2 tablespoons grated Parmigiano-Reggiano cheese

Venison
   2 tablespoons olive oil
   1 (2-pound) venison rack
   Salt and coarsely ground black pepper

Fried Sweet Potatoes
   1 cup peeled, thin matchstick strips of sweet potatoes
   1 quart oil for deep frying

Heat the demi-glace in a saucepan over medium heat and add the sliced black figs. Stir to mix well. Remove from the heat and reserve.

Preheat the oven to 350°F. Peel the sweet potatoes and slice paper thin. Toss in a bowl with the heavy cream. Add the butter and season with salt, white pepper and allspice. Pack in a buttered 8-inch x 8-inch ovenproof baking pan or into individual buttered molds. Cover with aluminum foil and place in the oven. Cook for 40 minutes. Remove the foil, sprinkle with cheese and place back into the oven until the cheese is melted.

Increase the oven to 400°F. Heat the oil in a large pan over medium high heat. Season the venison and sear on all sides in the hot pan. Place the venison on a rack and transfer to the oven and cook 20 to 25 minutes for medium-rare.

While the venison is cooking, heat one quart of oil in a deep-sided fry pan or deep fryer heated to 375°F and fry the sweet potatoes until golden brown. This will only take a couple of minutes. Remove and drain on absorbent paper. Reserve.

When the venison is done, remove from the oven. Cut into 4 portions, 2 ribs per serving.

Serve with sweet potatoes and black fig demi-glace. Serves 4

CHOCOLATE PECAN PIE WITH CHOCOLATE GRAVY

Grady Spears, Reata Restaurants, Alpine/Fort Worth

Pecan is an Algonquian word that means "hard shell" or "nuts requiring a stone to crack." As early as the 1500s, Spanish explorers found Native Americans using pecans to flavor their food. Texas is one of the major pecan-producing states, and the pecan, the only major nut tree that is native to North America, is the state tree. The nuts are kitchen favorites, especially for use in desserts like this one, a popular pie with Southern roots. Pronounce it "puh-kahn" (not "pee-can") and they'll think you're a native Texan. For white chocolate gravy, substitute white chocolate for the dark chocolate.

4 (4-inch) unbaked tart shells, or 1 (9-inch) unbaked pie shell

Chocolate Gravy

$^3/_4$ **pound dark chocolate, grated**
1 cup heavy whipping cream
$^1/_2$ **cup light corn syrup**
$^1/_2$ **cup sugar**
$^1/_2$ **cup unsalted butter, diced**

Pie

4 eggs
$^1/_3$ **cup sugar**
$^1/_3$ **cup all-purpose flour**
2 cups dark corn syrup
1 cup chocolate gravy
$^1/_2$ **teaspoon kosher salt**
$1^1/_2$ **cups pecan halves**

Vanilla ice cream

To make the **chocolate gravy**, place the grated chocolate in a mixing bowl. In a saucepan, combine the cream, corn syrup, and sugar and heat to 180°F. Pour the heated mixture over the chocolate and stir until the chocolate has completely melted. Fold in the butter until it has melted and is well incorporated. Reserve.

To make the **pie**, preheat the oven to 375°F. Place the eggs in a bowl and beat until pale yellow by hand or with a mixer. Gradually add the sugar and flour, beating until well incorporated. Fold in the corn syrup, 1 cup of the chocolate gravy, salt, and pecans. Pour the mixture into the tart shells or pie shell. Bake until the filling has set, about 1 hour. Transfer to a rack to cool.

To serve, top each wedge of pie or each tart with a scoop of ice cream and drizzle the remaining chocolate gravy over the top. Serves 4 to 6.

BUTTER PECAN ICE CREAM

Texas is a national leader in the consumption of ice cream. Its premier ice cream company, Blue Bell Creamery, in Brenham, has been churning out all kinds of flavors since 1911. If you aren't in Texas and want to make your own, this is a fabulous old-fashioned ice-cream recipe made from a rich custard base and a healthy portion of pecans. The ice cream is so addictive that you will want to double the recipe. Full-flavored Molasses Cookies will complement the rich ice cream (see recipe, page 138).

1 vanilla bean, or 1 tablespoon vanilla extract
2 cups milk
1$\frac{1}{4}$ cups heavy cream
$\frac{3}{4}$ cup sugar
9 egg yolks
3 tablespoons butter
1 cup pecan halves
$\frac{1}{4}$ teaspoon salt

What goes best with rich, buttery pecan ice cream? Spicy Molasses Cookies, of course—you'll find the recipe on page 138.

Split the vanilla bean in half lengthwise and, using the tip of a knife, scrape the seeds into a heavy saucepan. If using vanilla extract, reserve to use later. Add the pod halves, milk, cream, and sugar and place over medium heat. Heat, stirring to dissolve the sugar, until the milk is scalded. Remove from the heat and set aside. Meanwhile, in a small bowl, beat the egg yolks until pale yellow. Remove the vanilla bean from the cream mixture. Pour a small amount of the cream mixture into the yolks while stirring constantly. Add the tempered yolks to the cream mixture and cook over low heat, stirring constantly, until the mixture begins to thicken, about 8 minutes. Add vanilla extract if using. Remove the custard from the heat and set aside to cool.

In a skillet, melt the butter over medium heat. Add the pecans and salt and sauté until the nuts are toasted, about 5 minutes. Be careful not to burn the pecans. Stir the pecans into the custard.

Transfer the custard mixture to an ice-cream maker. Freeze according to the manufacturer's instructions.

Serve the ice cream with **molasses cookies**. Yields 1 quart.

GLAZED APPLE SPICE CAKE

Susan Molzan, Ruggles Grill, Houston

The apple industry in Texas goes mostly unnoticed, but in Texas Hill Country, the crop thrives. Apples make a statement in these moist cakes that rise high over the top of the oversized muffin tins. Serve a scoop of Mexican Vanilla Bean Ice Cream (see recipe, page 138) alongside and drizzle hot caramel sauce over the top.

Apple Spice Cake

- ¹/₂ pound (2 sticks) butter, at room temperature
- 1 cup vegetable oil
- 4 cups sugar
- 6 eggs, at room temperature
- 1 teaspoon vanilla extract
- 6 cups all-purpose flour
- 2 teaspoons ground cinnamon
- 1 tablespoon baking soda
- 1 teaspoon salt
- 7 Granny Smith apples, peeled and diced

Glaze

- ¹/₄ pound (1 stick) butter, at room temperature
- ¹/₂ pound cream cheese, at room temperature
- 3¹/₂ cups powdered sugar
- ¹/₂ teaspoon vanilla extract

Mexican Vanilla Bean Ice Cream (see recipe, page 138)

Hot Caramel Sauce

- 4 cups sugar
- 2 cups heavy cream

Preheat the oven to 350°F. Butter and flour twelve 4-inch muffin cups or popover molds. In a bowl or mixer, combine the butter, oil, and sugar and beat for 12 to 15 minutes on medium speed until smooth, creamy, and light. Lower the speed and add each egg. Add the vanilla and beat for 1 to 2 more minutes.

Gradually add the flour, cinnamon, soda, and salt, beating for 2 to 5 minutes until combined, stopping to scrape the sides of the bowl. Fold in the apples.

Spoon the batter into the muffin cups or molds to the rim. Bake until a toothpick inserted into the center of a muffin comes out clean, 45 to 60 minutes. Take the muffins out and place on a rack to cool.

To make the **glaze**, combine the butter and cream cheese and beat with a mixer on medium speed until blended. Add the powdered sugar and vanilla and beat until well blended, 4 to 6 minutes.

To make the **caramel sauce,** heat the sugar over medium low heat until it melts. Add ¹/₂ cup of water and stir constantly for 10 to 15 minutes over medium heat. Once the sugar has turned brown, add the cream and cook for 8 to 10 minutes more. Keep warm.

After the muffins have cooled for 30 to 40 minutes, spread some of the glaze on top of each of the muffins. Serve the muffins with a scoop of **vanilla ice cream** drizzled with the caramel sauce alongside. Makes 12 sizeable muffins.

BUÑUELOS AND MEXICAN HOT CHOCOLATE

A Mexican specialty, buñuelos are thin, crisp, slightly sweet pastries sprinkled with sugar and cinnamon. Served with Mexican hot chocolate, they are a San Antonio tradition at Christmas and New Years. If you yearn for them at other times of the year and don't want to make them yourself, Buñuelos, Inc, is a San Antonio factory where you can buy them year-round. Store leftovers in an airtight container.

Buñuelos

2 cups all-purpose flour
$\frac{1}{2}$ teaspoon baking powder
$\frac{1}{2}$ teaspoon salt
1 tablespoon plus $\frac{1}{2}$ cup sugar
2 tablespoons oil, plus vegetable oil for frying
1 tablespoon ground cinnamon

Mexican Hot Chocolate

2 ounces semisweet chocolate
2 tablespoons sugar
Pinch of salt
4 cups milk
4 tablespoons Kahlúa
$\frac{1}{2}$ cup heavy cream, whipped stiff
Ground cinnamon for sprinkling

To make the **buñuelos**, sift together the flour, baking powder, salt, and 1 tablespoon sugar into a bowl. Stir in the 2 tablespoons oil and then slowly add $\frac{1}{2}$ cup water while continuously stirring until the dough holds together. If the dough is too dry, add additional water. Place on a floured surface and knead the dough 1 to 2 minutes or until it is smooth and elastic. Add a little more flour if the dough is too tacky. Divide the dough into 16 to 20 balls. Roll out each ball into a thin round about $\frac{1}{4}$-inch thick and 4 to 5 inches in diameter. Prick each round a few times with a fork and let rest for 10 minutes before cooking.

Pour oil to a depth of 1 to 2 inches into a deep skillet and heat to 350°F. In batches, add the dough rounds to the pan in a single layer and fry, turning once or twice, until golden brown on both sides. Using tongs, transfer to paper towels to drain. In a bowl, stir together the remaining $\frac{1}{2}$ cup sugar and the cinnamon and sprinkle on the buñuelos while they are still warm.

To make the **hot chocolate**, combine the chocolate, sugar, and salt in a heavy saucepan over medium-low heat and heat until the chocolate melts. Slowly stir in the milk and turn up the heat. Bring to a boil while stirring constantly. When the mixture begins to boil, add the Kahlúa, mixing well. Remove from the heat. Pour into mugs and top with a spoonful of whipped cream and a sprinkling of cinnamon.

Serve the buñuelos warm or at room temperature with the hot chocolate. Makes 16 to 20 buñuelos, and 4 servings of hot chocolate.

HEAVEN AND HELL CAKE

Stephan Pyles, Star Canyon, Dallas

This is one of the most decadent layer cakes you'll ever taste. It makes an impressive and absolutely delicious special occasion dessert with two ingredients that people have always loved—chocolate and peanut butter. Give it a try when you have the time to make it. You won't be sorry.

Angel Food Cake
1⅓ cups cake flour
2 cups powdered sugar
2 cups egg whites (about 14–16)
Pinch of salt
2 teaspoons cream of tartar
1⅓ cups sugar
2 teaspoons vanilla extract
1 teaspoon almond extract

Devil's Food Cake
½ cup cocoa powder
1 cup strong coffee
½ cup shortening
1½ cups sugar
1 teaspoon vanilla extract
2 eggs
1½ cups cake flour
¾ teaspoon salt
¼ teaspoon baking powder
1 teaspoon baking soda

Peanut Butter Mousse
12 ounces cream cheese
1¾ cups powdered sugar
2 cups peanut butter, room temperature
¾ cup heavy cream, whipped stiff

Ganache
2 cups cream
2 pounds milk chocolate, chopped

Make the **angel food cake**. Cut a circle of parchment paper or waxed paper to fit the bottom of an ungreased 10-inch cake pan. Preheat the oven to 375°F.

Sift together the flour and powdered sugar and set aside. Place the egg whites in the bowl of a heavy-duty mixer. Beat slowly while adding the salt and cream of tartar and continue beating for 2 minutes. Increase the speed to medium and pour the sugar into the whites by tablespoons until it is all incorporated. Continue to beat for about 3 minutes longer. When the egg whites have stiff peaks, add the vanilla and almond extracts.

Remove the bowl from the mixer and sprinkle half of the powdered sugar-flour mixture over the top of the egg whites and fold in with a rubber spatula. Sprinkle with the remaining sugar-flour mixture and fold in again, using a minimum number of strokes so the egg whites to not deflate. Gently spoon the mixture into the pan and bake for 1 hour. Remove from the oven and set aside to cool.

(*Continued on page 139*)

PITAHAYA SORBET

Michael Cordua, Américas, Houston

The colorful blossoms that grow at the tip of cactus nodules develop into fruit called prickly pears, and these cactus pears have been a staple food of Native Americans for centuries. Pitahaya, or dragon fruit, has a vibrant magenta flesh and is a variety common to Central and South America. The pulp is sweet and lends itself well to fruit drinks, desserts, and sorbets. The frozen purée is sold in stores that specialize in Latin American foods. If unavailable, the more common variety of prickly pear may be substituted. Use gloves and take care when handling the fruit; they have tiny, almost invisible, bristles. If you're using the common variety, it is full of very hard seeds, so be sure to strain the seeds from the pulp.

Pitahaya Sorbet sits next to a Pitahaya Margarita at the Américas bar. See the recipe for the margarita on page 126.

1 cup pitahaya pulp
    (or 4 to 6 pitahaya or prickly pears)
1 cup water
1¼ cups sugar
½ cup fresh lime juice
1 egg white
Pinch of salt

Peel the pitahaya carefully and cut in chunks. Put into the blender and process until smooth. The tiny black seeds don't have to be removed.

Meanwhile, simmer the sugar with the water in a small skillet over medium heat for 1 to 2 minutes to dissolve the sugar. Remove the skillet from the heat and stir in the lime juice and the pitahaya puree.

Cool the mixture by pouring it into a bowl and setting it in a larger bowl of water with ice cubes. Or, cover and refrigerate.

In a mixing bowl, beat the egg whites with the salt until stiff, but not dry, and whisk into the cooled pitahaya mixture.

Pour the mixture into an ice cream machine and freeze according to the manufacturer's directions. Yields about 1 quart.

DRINKS

TEQUILA SUNRISE
Hunter Brothers' Ranch

Ice cubes
1½ ounces tequila

¼ ounce grenadine
¾ cup (6 ounces) fresh
orange juice

Fill a highball glass with ice cubes. Pour the tequila and the grenadine over the ice and top off with the orange juice. Yields 1 drink.

CHILE MARTINI
Hunter Brothers' Ranch

1 ounce pepper vodka
(Absolut peppar or
Stolichnaya pertsovka)

¼ ounce dry vermouth
1 jalapeño-stuffed olive

Combine the vodka and vermouth in a shaker filled with ice. Shake well, then strain into a martini glass and garnish with a jalapeño-stuffed olive. Yields 1 drink.

MARGARITA
Hunter Brothers' Ranch

1 lime wedge
Coarse salt
Cracked ice

1 ounce tequila
½ ounce Triple Sec
1 ounce fresh lime juice

Wet the rim of an old-fashioned glass by rubbing with the moist side of a lime wedge. Invert the glass and dip the rim into the salt. Shake off any excess salt from the glass and fill with ice. Combine the tequila, Triple Sec, lime juice, and ice in a shaker and shake well. Strain into the glass. Yields 1 drink.

FROZEN PEACH MARGARITA
Hunter Brothers' Ranch

1 lime wedge
(optional)
Sugar and salt for rim
(optional)
1 ounce tequila
1 ounce peach schnapps

1 ounce fresh lime juice
1 cup coarsely-chopped
frozen peach slices
¼ teaspoon sugar
½ ounce Triple Sec
¼ cup cracked ice

If desired, wet the rim of a margarita glass by rubbing with the moist side of a lime wedge, invert the glass, and dip the rim into salt or sugar and shake off any excess. Put all of the remaining ingredients into a blender and purée until smooth. Serve in the margarita glass. Yields 1 drink.

PITAHAYA MARGARITA
Michael Cordua, Américas, Houston
(see photo, page 125)

¼ cup pitahaya sorbet
¼ cup fresh lime juice
2 tablespoons Triple Sec

2 ounces tequila
1 cup crushed ice or cubes

Put all of the ingredients into a blender and purée on high speed until firm. Pour into pre-chilled cocktail glasses. If making a larger quantity, mix the ingredients together in a pitcher and blend in batches. Yields 2 drinks.

ADDITIONAL RECIPES

CHARRO BEANS

1 pound dried pinto beans, rinsed, soaked
   overnight, and drained
$^1/_2$ pound smoked pork sausage, cut into 1-inch
   pieces
1 cup chopped onion
$^1/_2$ cup chopped green bell pepper
5 garlic cloves, minced
2 jalapeño chiles, seeded and minced
1 ($14^1/_2$-ounce) can chopped tomatoes
3 tablespoons chopped fresh cilantro
1 tablespoon brown sugar
3 tablespoons chile powder compound
2 tablespoons ground cumin
$^1/_2$ teaspoon dried oregano
$1^1/_2$ teaspoons salt
$^1/_2$ teaspoon freshly ground pepper
2 bay leaves

Place beans in a large pot along with 2 quarts water
and all the remaining ingredients. Bring to a boil,
reduce the heat to low, and simmer uncovered,
stirring occasionally, until the beans are tender and
thick, about 2 hours. Remove the bay leaves before
serving. Yields about 2 quarts, for 8 servings.

POTATO–WHITE BEAN PURÉE

1 medium-sized potato, peeled and diced
1 tablespoon extra-virgin olive oil
$^1/_4$ cup chopped shallot
2 tablespoons minced garlic
1 cup cooked white beans
6 tablespoons sour cream
6 tablespoons heavy cream

Salt and freshly ground pepper to taste
$1^1/_2$ teaspoons chopped fresh thyme
$1^1/_2$ teaspoons chopped fresh oregano

Boil the potato until tender in salted water, drain,
and put through a ricer or mash until smooth. In a
small skillet, heat the oil over medium heat. Add the
shallot and cook until tender but not brown. Add the
garlic and white beans and cook until the garlic is
tender, 2 to 3 minutes. In a blender, combine the
beans and potatoes and purée until smooth, then
pour into a bowl. Add the sour cream and heavy
cream and blend well. Season with salt and pepper.
Allow to cool slightly, and add the herbs. Allow to
thicken by refrigerating overnight.

BLACK BEANS

1 pound dried black beans, rinsed, soaked
   overnight, and drained
1 (6-ounce) slab apple-smoked bacon, cubed
1 carrot
1 large onion stuck with 3 whole cloves
3 garlic cloves
1 *bouquet garni*, made with $^1/_2$ bunch fresh
   thyme, 1 bay leaf, a few fresh parsley stems,
   and 8 peppercorns, wrapped in cheesecloth
Kosher salt

Place beans in a large pot along with the bacon,
carrot, onion pierced with cloves, garlic cloves, and
one bouquet garni. Season with salt and add water
to cover. Bring to a boil, then reduce the heat to low
and simmer until the beans are cooked but still firm,

25 to 30 minutes. Remove and discard the carrot, onion, and *bouquet garni* from the beans.

BLACK-EYED PEA RELISH

$^1\!/_2$ cup fresh shelled black-eyed peas,
     cooked and cooled
$^1\!/_3$ cup corn kernels cut from grilled corn
     on the cob
$^1\!/_3$ cup matchstick-cut red onion
$^1\!/_2$ roasted red bell pepper, diced
2 green onions (white and green parts),
     finely chopped
1 tablespoon chopped fresh chives
1 tablespoon chopped fresh cilantro
1 tablespoon chopped fresh thyme
1 teaspoon minced garlic
1 teaspoon seeded, minced jalapeño chile
Juice of 1 lime
1 tablespoon extra-virgin olive oil
1 tablespoon olive oil
1 tablespoon balsamic vinegar
Salt and freshly ground pepper to taste

Combine all of the ingredients in a bowl and mix well. Cover and let stand at room temperature for at least 1 hour to blend the flavors (this can also be refrigerated overnight).

BUNKHOUSE BAKED BEANS

$^1\!/_2$ pound sliced smoked bacon
1 cup chopped onion
3 garlic cloves, minced
3 tablespoon minced jalapeño chile
2 cups (1 pound) cooked pinto beans,
     or 6 cups canned and drained beans
$^3\!/_4$ cup chile sauce
$^1\!/_2$ cup plus 2 tablespoons molasses
2 tablespoons mustard

1 tablespoon cider vinegar
$^3\!/_4$ teaspoon salt
$^1\!/_4$ teaspoon freshly ground black pepper
$^1\!/_4$ teaspoon Tabasco or other hot sauce

Fry the bacon strips until crisp to render drippings. Remove the bacon and drain on paper towels. In the drippings, sauté the onions, garlic, and chile. Combine the pinto beans, sautéed vegetables, and the remaining ingredients in a 3-quart casserole. Crumble the bacon into small pieces and sprinkle on top of the beans and cover with $1^1\!/_2$ cups of water. Cover the casserole and bake at 350°F for $1^1\!/_2$ hours until they have thickened. Serve warm. Yields about 7 cups.

SPANISH RICE

$^1\!/_4$ cup olive oil
1 cup long-grain white rice
$^1\!/_2$ cup chopped onion
$^1\!/_2$ cup chopped green bell pepper
2 garlic cloves, minced
1 ripe tomato, chopped (about 1 cup)
2 tablespoons minced fresh cilantro
2 tablespoons minced fresh parsley
$1^1\!/_2$ cups chicken stock
$^3\!/_4$ teaspoon salt
$^1\!/_4$ teaspoon freshly ground pepper

In a heavy saucepan, heat the olive oil over medium heat. Stir in the rice, making sure it is coated with oil, and brown for 5 to 6 minutes. Add the onion, bell pepper, and garlic and sauté until the onion is tender, about 5 minutes longer. Add all of the remaining ingredients, stir well, and bring the mixture to a boil. Reduce the heat to low, cover, and cook until all of the stock is absorbed, about 20 minutes. Serves about 6.

TEXMATI RICE

2 cups Texmati or basmati rice
$^3/_4$ teaspoon saffron threads
$^1/_2$ teaspoon salt
$^1/_2$ teaspoon safflower or vegetable oil
$^1/_2$ teaspoon black mustard seeds

Rinse the rice in 7 or 8 changes of water, then cover with water and let soak for 10 minutes. Drain and place in a large, heavy saucepan along with the saffron, salt, and 4 cups of cold water. Bring to a boil over high heat, stir once, and reduce the heat to low. Cover and cook until the liquid is absorbed and the rice is tender, 15 to 20 minutes. Remove from the heat, uncover, and fluff with a fork. Re-cover to keep warm. Meanwhile, heat the oil in a small skillet. Add a mustard seed. If it pops immediately, the oil is ready. Add the remaining seeds to the oil, cover the pan, and heat the seeds until they all pop. Pour the seeds over the rice.

TEX-MEX CORNBREAD

2 eggs
4 tablespoons butter, melted
1 ($8^1/_2$-ounce) can cream-style corn
1 cup sour cream
1 cup yellow cornmeal
3 jalapeño chiles, seeded and minced
$^1/_2$ cup chopped onion
3 tablespoons chopped jarred pimento
4 teaspoons baking powder
$^3/_4$ teaspoon salt
1 cup (4 ounces) shredded sharp cheddar
   cheese

Put a well-oiled 9-inch cast-iron skillet into a cold oven and heat the oven to 400°F. Meanwhile, in a large bowl, combine the eggs and butter and work together with a fork. Stir in all the remaining ingredients until well mixed.

Carefully remove the skillet from the oven and pour the batter into the hot pan. Return the pan to the oven and bake until firm to the touch, about 1 hour. The crust will be a deep golden brown. Cut into wedges and serve hot. Serves 8.

CREAMY WHITE GRITS

$1^1/_4$ cups coarse white grits
$1^1/_2$ teaspoons salt

Bring 4 cups water to a boil in a heavy 2-quart saucepan. Add the grits and salt while stirring constantly. Bring the water back to a boil, then reduce the heat to a very low simmer. Cover and cook until the grits are very thick, stirring every 2 or 3 minutes. The grits will be ready in about 20 minutes. If the grits become too thick, add a little water to adjust the consistency. Keep warm until ready to serve.

CAT HEAD BISCUITS

So-named because they are the size of a cat's head.

2 cups flour
1 tablespoon baking powder
$^1/_2$ teaspoon baking soda
$1^1/_2$ teaspoons sugar
$^1/_2$ teaspoon salt
$^1/_3$ cup shortening
1 cup buttermilk

In a large mixing bowl sift together the dry ingredients. Cut the shortening into the flour mixture using a pastry cutter until completely incorporated. Stir in the buttermilk until the mixture holds together. Remove the dough from the bowl and knead on a floured surface turning three or four times. Do not overwork the dough. Divide the dough into ten equal portions. Roll each portion into a ball and place on an ungreased cookie sheet. Press the dough balls flat until about two and one-half to three inches in diameter. Bake in a preheated 450°F oven for 10 to 12 minutes or until golden brown. Yields 10 biscuits.

POLENTA

Freshly ground pepper to taste
1 bay leaf
$^3/_4$ cup polenta
$^1/_4$ cup sliced mixed seasonal mushrooms (available packaged in markets), steamed until tender
1 ounce dry pack sun-dried tomatoes, soaked in warm water until softened, drained, and diced
1 tablespoon equal parts chopped fresh *fines herbes* (chervil, chives, parsley, and tarragon)
Mist of canola or olive oil for pan searing

Combine 2 cups water, the pepper, and the bay leaf in a medium-size cast-iron saucepan and bring to a simmer. Very slowly sift the polenta into the pan through the fingers of one hand, stirring constantly with a wooden spoon. Reduce the heat to medium-low and continue to stir constantly until the polenta is smooth and thick and pulls away from the sides of the pan, about 30 minutes. Discard the bay leaf and fold in the steamed mushrooms, sun-dried tomatoes and herbs, mixing all of the ingredients together. Spread the mixture about $^1/_4$-inch deep on a parchment-lined pan and smooth the surface with a rubber spatula dipped in water. Refrigerate the polenta until firmly set.

Preheat the oven to 350°F. Turn the polenta out of the pan and cut it into 12 diamonds. Mist a cast iron skillet with canola–olive oil blend and place over medium heat. In batches if necessary, place the polenta diamonds in the pan and fry, turning once, until golden on both sides. Tranfer the polenta to a baking pan and place in the oven until heated through, 3 to 4 minutes.

BARBECUED VENISON FAJITAS

1$^1/_2$ teaspoons olive oil
1 poblano pepper, seeds and stems removed, and cut into thin strips
1 medium red onion, cut into thin strips
1 (6 ounce) portion of venison loin, trimmed of fat and silver skin, cut into thin strips
Salt and freshly ground pepper
$^1/_2$ cup of your favorite barbecue sauce
$^1/_4$ cup grated jalapeno-jack cheese
4 (6 inch) corn tortillas, warmed

Heat oil in a medium sauté pan over medium-high heat. Add the poblano pepper and onion and sauté for one minute, leaving the onion crunchy. Season the venison strips with salt and pepper, add to the pan and sauté for one minute to quickly brown the meat. Add the barbecue sauce. Remove from the heat and stir in the cheese until well-incorporated into the sauce. Spoon the mixture onto the center of each tortilla and roll into a cylinder. Keep warm. Serves 4.

YELLOW TOMATO–POZOLE STEW

4 large yellow tomatoes, left whole
1 tablespoon olive oil
1 poblano chile, stem removed, seeded and cut
    into large dice
1 large onion, cut into large dice
1 cup diced celery (large dice)
3 garlic cloves, minced
1 jalapeño chile, cut into small dice
2 teaspoons ground cumin
2 teaspoons ground coriander
$^1/_4$ cup gold tequila
$^1/_2$ cup beer
2 cups rich chicken stock
4 corn tortillas, fried
Salt and freshly ground pepper to taste
Fresh lime juice
1 tablespoon olive oil
$^1/_4$ cup diced country ham
$^1/_2$ cup fresh corn kernels
$^1/_4$ cup diced red onion
$^1/_4$ cup diced celery
1 tablespoon finely diced jalapeño chile
$^3/_4$ cup pozole, cooked
$^1/_4$ cup diced yellow tomato
$^1/_4$ cup diced red tomato

Place the tomatoes on a baking sheet and roast in a 375°F oven until soft, about 15 minutes. Remove from the oven and purée in a blender until smooth. Set aside. In a heavy saucepan, heat the oil over medium-high heat. Add the poblano chile, onion, and celery and sauté until the onion is translucent, about 3 minutes. Add the garlic, jalapeño, cumin, and coriander and sauté for 1 minute. Deglaze the pan with the tequila and beer, scraping to loosen any browned bits from the pan. Cook over medium high heat until reduced by one-half, about 1 minute.

Add the chicken stock, tortillas, and reserved tomatoes. Bring the mixture to a boil over high heat, reduce the heat to low, and simmer until thickened, about 20 minutes. Strain through a large-hole strainer and season with salt, pepper, and lime juice to taste. Reserve.

To finish the stew, heat the olive oil in a heavy saucepan over medium-high heat. Add the ham and sauté until browned, about 2 minutes. Add the corn, onion, celery, and jalapeño and sauté until the onion is translucent, about 3 minutes. Add the remaining ingredients and heat through. Add the reserved tomato mixture and mix well.

CONFETTI CORN

5 tablespoons unsalted butter, at room
    temperature
3 tablespoons chopped jarred pimento
$^3/_4$ teaspoon ground cumin
$^1/_4$ teaspoon chile powder
2 tablespoons diced red bell pepper
2 tablespoons diced green bell pepper
2 tablespoons thinly sliced green onions
4 cups fresh or frozen corn kernels, cooked
Salt to taste

In a skillet, melt the butter over medium heat. Add all of the remaining ingredients except the corn and salt and sauté until just tender. Stir in the corn, mix well, and heat through. Season with salt and serve immediately. Serves 4 to 6.

STEWED OKRA AND TOMATOES

2 tablespoons butter
1 shallot, minced
1 garlic clove, minced
2 tomatoes, chopped
2 cups sliced fresh okra
$\frac{1}{4}$ cup thinly sliced fresh basil
Salt and freshly ground pepper

Melt the butter in a saucepan over medium heat and add the shallot and garlic. Sweat the vegetables a few minutes until tender. Add the tomatoes and okra. Cover and simmer for 45 minutes to 1 hour until the tomatoes have released all of their juices. Just before serving, stir in the basil. Add salt and pepper to taste. Serves 4.

OUTLAW COLESLAW WITH RUBY RED GRAPEFRUIT AND PINEAPPLE

If you decide to use fresh pineapple, measure out 1 cup chopped, then put it in a blender and pulse very briefly to crush it.

2 pounds cabbage, shredded
1 (8-ounce can) crushed pineapple, undrained
1 Ruby Red grapefruit, peeled and sectioned
$\frac{1}{4}$ cup mayonnaise
$1\frac{1}{2}$ teaspoons white vinegar
1 tablespoon sugar
$\frac{1}{8}$ teaspoon white pepper
$\frac{1}{2}$ teaspoon salt

Combine all of the ingredients in a large bowl and mix well. Chill before serving. Makes 1 quart. Serves 6.

ROASTED CORN ON THE COB WITH JALAPEÑO–LIME BUTTER

$\frac{1}{2}$ cup (1 stick) unsalted butter, at room temperature
1 tablespoon fresh lime juice
2 teaspoons grated lime zest
$1\frac{1}{2}$ teaspoons minced jalapeño chile
$\frac{1}{2}$ teaspoon salt

6 to 8 ears corn in the husk

To prepare the butter, combine all of the ingredients in a bowl and beat until well combined. You will have about $\frac{1}{2}$ cup. To shape the butter into uniform rounds, scoop it out onto a piece of plastic wrap and shape it into a log $1\frac{1}{2}$ inches in diameter. Chill well. When firm, slice the butter into $\frac{1}{4}$-inch thick slices.

Peel back the husk of the ears of corn, but do not detach, and remove all the silk. Replace the husks around the ears, and then soak the ears in cold water to cover for about 1 hour.

Prepare a smoker. When ready to cook, drain the corn. Pull back the husk on each ear, spread the kernels with jalapeño-lime butter, and re-cover the ear with the husk. Put the corn in the preheated smoker and cook for $1\frac{1}{2}$ hours.

Alternatively, prepare the corn as above and wrap each ear in a double-thickness of aluminum foil and twist the ends to seal. Put the ears on a low-to-medium hot grill and cook, turning often, for about 20 minutes. Serve the corn hot. Serves 6.

ONION RINGS

3 onions, spiral cut or cut into rings
1 cup flour
$1/4$ cup paprika
$1/4$ cup pure chile powder
$1/4$ cup toasted cumin seeds, ground
2 teaspoons cayenne pepper
Milk for soaking the onions
Salt to taste

Combine the dry ingredients, except for the salt, in a bowl. In another bowl, soak the sliced onions in milk, then shake off the excess milk when ready to cook. Toss the slices in the flour mixture until well coated. Heat canola oil to 360 ° F and fry the onions a few at a time until golden, about 45 seconds. Remove from the oil and drain. Season with salt.

GERMAN BACON-LACED POTATO SALAD

$1 1/2$ pounds potatoes, unpeeled (about 4)
6 strips bacon
2 tablespoons reserved bacon drippings
1 onion, finely chopped
1 teaspoon sugar
$1/2$ teaspoon celery seed
$1/2$ cup cider vinegar
Salt and freshly ground pepper

In a large pot of water, boil the potatoes 15 to 20 minutes, or until tender. Drain and set the potatoes aside to cool.

While the potatoes are cooking, fry the bacon in a skillet over medium heat until crisp. Remove from the pan and drain on paper towels. Reserve 2 tablespoons of bacon drippings. Crumble the bacon and set aside.

Combine the bacon drippings, onion, sugar, celery seed, and vinegar together in a bowl and mix well. When the potatoes are cool enough to handle, peel and cut into bite-size chunks. Pour the bacon dripping mixture over the potatoes and toss. Season with salt and pepper and sprinkle with crumbled bacon. This potato salad is served warm or at room temperature. Serves 4.

SWEET POTATOES

2 large sweet potatoes, peeled and diced
$1/2$ white potato, peeled and diced
6 tablespoons maple syrup
2 teaspoons salt
1 teaspoon cayenne powder
1 tablespoon pure chile powder
8 tablespoons (1 stick) unsalted butter, room temperature

In a saucepan, bring the potatoes to a boil, reduce the heat and simmer for 15 minutes until soft. Drain and transfer the potatoes to a food processor. Add the maple syrup, salt, cayenne and chile powder. Process for 1 minute while adding the butter a tablespoon at a time. Keep warm in a pan until ready to serve.

SPINACH RAITA

4 cups (1 quart) plain yogurt, strained in a colander in the refrigerator overnight
$1 1/2$ teaspoons chopped garlic
$1 1/2$ teaspoons chopped ginger root
1 cup packed spinach leaves well rinsed
$1/2$ jalapeño chile, seeded and chopped
$1 1/2$ to 3 teaspoons fresh lemon juice, or to taste

1½ teaspoons honey
Cayenne pepper to taste
Salt and freshly ground black pepper to taste

Combine all of the ingredients except ½ cup of the spinach in a blender and purée until smooth. Finely chop the remaining spinach and stir into the mixture. Cover and refrigerate until ready to use.

CHILCOSTLE SAUCE

2 tablespoons butter
½ cup chopped white onion
6 garlic cloves
1 plum tomato, about ¼ pound, chopped
2 chilcostle chiles, seeded, stemmed, roasted
¼ small fennel bulb, tops discarded, chopped (optional)
A few saffron threads (optional)
3 cups strained fish stock, clam broth or reconstituted fish bouillion
1 large fresh tarragon sprig or hoja santa leaf
1 cup heavy cream
Salt and freshly ground pepper to taste

Melt the butter in a saucepan over low heat. Add all of the ingredients except the broth, tarragon, cream, salt, and pepper in sauté pan and sauté, stirring frequently, for about 3 to 5 minutes. Do not brown or burn the ingredients. Try to achieve a light brick-red color. Continue to cook until all of the liquid has evaporated, about 6 to 8 minutes. Add the broth and the tarragon sprig and simmer until the ingredients are tender, about 15 minutes. Add the heavy cream and simmer an additional 15 minutes. Discard the tarragon sprig. Transfer the contents of the pan to a blender and purée until smooth. Strain the sauce and season. Keep warm until used.

LENTILS WITH DRIED APRICOTS

1 tablespoon olive oil
6 garlic cloves, chopped
2 onions, chopped
4 cups French lentils, rinsed and picked over
4 teaspoons salt
1 tablespoon sliced dried apricots
1 tablespoon chopped fresh thyme
1 tablespoon minced ginger root

Heat the oil over medium heat in a saucepan. Add the garlic and onions and sauté until caramelized, about 8 to 10 minutes. Add the lentils, 2 quarts water, and salt and bring to a boil. Reduce the heat to low and simmer uncovered for 15 minutes or until lentils are tender. Drain lentils and return to the pan. Add the apricots, thyme, and ginger, toss well, and return to low heat to heat through.

TUMBLEWEED BARBECUE SAUCE

1 cup ketchup
1 cup chile sauce
1 cup beer
1 large onion, roughly chopped
2 garlic cloves, finely chopped
3 tablespoons Worcestershire sauce
2 tablespoons cider vinegar
Juice of 1 lime
1 tablespoon chile powder
1 tablespoon black pepper

In a heavy sauce pan, mix together all ingredients and simmer for 30 minutes, stirring from time to time. With a slotted spoon, remove the onions and garlic from the sauce and put into a blender. Process until smooth and return the purée to the barbecue sauce. Mix well. Makes about 4½ cups.

CABERNET GLAZE

1 tablespoon canola oil
$\frac{1}{4}$ pound beef cubes
2 shallots, diced
1 carrot, finely diced
2 cups red wine, preferably Cabernet
    Sauvignon
2 teaspoons finely chopped fresh Mexican
    marigold mint or tarragon
$\frac{1}{4}$ cup dried porcini mushrooms, soaked in $\frac{1}{2}$ cup
    chicken stock
1 cup rich duck and/or veal stock
4 tablespoons unsalted butter, cut into small
    pieces
Kosher salt and freshly ground pepper to taste

Preheat a medium-size saucepan over medium heat for 2 minutes and add the oil and beef cubes. Cook, stirring constantly for about 5 minutes to brown the cubes on all sides. Add the shallots and carrot and continue cooking for 4 minutes, stirring constantly and scraping up any browned bits clinging to the pan. Add the red wine and deglaze, stirring to release any additional meat glaze on the pan. Transfer the contents of the pan to a small saucepan and return to medium heat. Add the Mexican marigold mint and porcini mushrooms to the stock. Add the duck and/or veal stock and bring to a boil. Reduce the heat to low and simmer until reduced by one-half, about 30 minutes. Strain through a fine-mesh strainer into a clean saucepan. Continue to simmer and reduce by one-third more, or until smooth and shiny. Whisk in the butter, a piece at a time. Season with salt and pepper.

COWBOY RUB

$\frac{1}{2}$ cup kosher salt
1 cup pure chile powder
1 cup paprika
$\frac{1}{3}$ cup sugar

Combine all ingredients. Great on Rib-eye steak!

GARLIC-RED CHILE OIL

$\frac{1}{2}$ cup olive oil
1 tablespoon chopped garlic
1 chipotle chile
1 teaspoon chile powder
Juice of 1 lime
1 teaspoon chopped fresh thyme
Salt and freshly ground pepper to taste

Heat 1 tablespoon of the olive oil in a small skillet over low heat. Add the garlic and sauté until tender but not brown, about 2 minutes. Heat the chipotle chile in a dry skillet over medium temp until it is soft and flexible, about 3 minutes. Remove from the heat and, when cool enough to handle, remove the seeds and tear into pieces. Heat the chile powder in a dry skillet over low heat for 1 minute to develop the flavors. Remove from the heat. Put the garlic, chipotle, chile powder, and lime juice in the blender and purée, drizzling in the remaining olive oil with the blender running. Add the thyme, season with salt and pepper and purée until smooth. Cover and refrigerate until used.

OSTRICH MOP

$^1/_2$ cup balsamic vinegar
3 tablespoons dried *herbes de Provence*
1 teaspoon freshly ground pepper
1 teaspoon kosher salt
1 teaspoon New Mexico chile powder
$^1/_4$ cup dried porcini mushrooms, ground to a
    powder in a spice mill
$^1/_4$ cup maple syrup
$^1/_4$ cup molasses
1 cup walnut oil
1 cup olive oil

Combine the vinegar, *herbes de Provence*, pepper, salt, chile powder, and porcini powder. Whisk vigorously to combine. Whisk in the maple syrup and molasses. Whisk in the oils in a slow, steady stream.

CITRUS SALAD
WITH APPLE CIDER VINAIGRETTE

8 shallots, finely chopped
2 tablespoons finely chopped thyme
$^1/_2$ cup apple butter (store-bought)
6 tablespoons cider vinegar
$^3/_4$ cup olive oil
Salt and freshly ground pepper
2 oranges, sectioned
2 grapefruits, sectioned
2 lemons, sectioned
4 cups salad greens

Mix the first 4 ingredients together in a mixing bowl. Slowly whisk or blend in the oil and season with salt and pepper to taste. Set aside.

To section each fruit, cut a slice from the top and from the bottom. Cut off the peel in strips from top to bottom, cutting deep enough to remove the white pith. Cut along the side of each dividing membrane from outside to the middle of the fruit core, removing the sections. Cut each fruit section in half, and toss with the salad greens and dressing.

PASILLA CHILE BROTH

1 tablespoon butter
$^1/_2$ (8-ounce) large white onion, coarsely chopped
4 to 8 garlic cloves, peeled and left whole
2 pasilla chiles (about $^1/_2$ ounce total), stems
    removed, seeded, and torn into large pieces
1 ($^3/_4$-ounce) thick, white corn tortilla
2 $^1/_2$ cups chicken stock
1/4 cup heavy cream
1 teaspoon coarse salt
1 teaspoon brown sugar

Melt the butter in a saucepan over medium-high heat. Add the onion and garlic and sauté for a few minutes until nicely browned. Add the chile and tortilla pieces and sauté slowly until the ingredients are golden brown, reducing the heat to medium-low if necessary. This should take about 5 to 6 minutes. Add the chicken stock, bring to a boil, reduce the heat to low, cover partially, and simmer for about 10 minutes. Remove from the heat and let cool. Transfer the contents of the pan to a blender and purée until smooth, about 1 minute. Pass the sauce through a strainer into a clean pan. Stir in the cream, salt, and brown sugar until well blended. The sauce should not be too thick. Add some additional stock or water to thin if necessary. Reserve and keep warm until ready to serve.

LAMB-BRAISING LIQUID

Olive oil for sautéeing
1 cup diced carrot
1 cup diced celery
1 cup diced onion
4 cups dry red wine
2 tablespoons tomato paste
3 bay leaves

Heat a little olive oil in a large skillet over medium heat. Add the carrot, celery, and onion and sauté until caramelized, about 8 to 10 minutes. Add the red wine, tomato paste, and bay leaves. Raise the heat to high, and bring to a boil. Reduce the heat to a simmer for 10 minutes to blend the flavors.

BANANA MOJO

1 tablespoon butter
1 small banana, diced
$1/4$ cup minced red onion
$1/4$ cup minced green bell pepper
$1/2$ teaspoon minced garlic
1 tablespoon minced green onion
$1/2$ teaspoon minced habañero chile
1 tablespoon yellow mustard seeds
1 tablespoon brown sugar
1 teaspoon Dijon mustard
$1^1/2$ teaspoons fresh orange juice
1 tablespoon Champagne vinegar

Melt the butter in a sauté pan over medium heat. Add the banana and sauté until tender, about 2 to 3 minutes. Reduce the heat to low and add the red onion, bell pepper, garlic, green onion and habañero chile. Cover and sweat the vegetables about 5 minutes, until they release their juices, but not allow them to brown. Add the mustard seeds, brown sugar and Dijon mustard and mix well. Add the orange juice and vinegar and simmer briefly to blend flavors. Set aside and keep warm.

MATOKE MASH

1 medium ripe yellow plantain, peeled and sliced
2 medium Russet potatoes, diced
3 tablespoons unsalted butter
$1/2$ -$3/4$ cup half and half, warmed
Salt and freshly ground pepper to taste

Place the sliced plantain and potatoes in a large pot and cover by at least 1 inch with salted water. Simmer for approximately 30 minutes or until tender. Drain the plantain and potatoes in a colander and force them through a food mill or ricer. Add the butter and fold in the warm half and half. Season with salt and pepper. Set aside and keep warm.

PEPIAN

2 large tomatillos, husk removed, washed and quartered
$1/2$ cup diced yellow onion
$1/4$ cup roughly chopped fresh cilantro
2 garlic cloves, minced
$1^1/2$ teaspoons minced jalapeño chile
1 tablespoon chopped, fresh oregano
$1/4$ cup fresh spinach, washed, fried, stems removed
1 tablespoon butter
2 tablespoons shelled pumpkin seeds
$1/4$ cup diakon sprouts (optional)
Salt and freshly ground pepper

Put the pumpkin seeds on a baking sheet and toast in a preheated 350°F oven for 7 to 10 minutes to bring out the flavors and slightly brown. Remove and when cool, grind in a spice mill until fine-textured. Combine the ingredients except for the butter, pumpkin seeds, salt and pepper in a blender and purée. Season to taste. Pour the mixture into a medium saucepot over medium heat. Bring to a simmer and add the butter and pumpkin seeds. Stir until the butter melts, and adjust the seasoning. Serve as soon as possible to retain the bright green color.

SAGE PESTO

1 cup fresh sage leaves, coarsely chopped
$\frac{1}{2}$ cup fresh Italian parsley leaves, coarsely chopped
$\frac{1}{2}$ teaspoon chopped shallot
$\frac{1}{4}$ teaspoon chopped garlic
Juice of $\frac{1}{2}$ lemon
$\frac{1}{2}$ cup olive oil
Salt and freshly ground pepper to taste

Place the sage, parsley, shallot, garlic, and lemon juice in a blender. Add a splash of water and purée until smooth. Once the mixture starts to smooth out, drizzle in the oil. Purée until smooth and season.

MOLASSES COOKIES

4 cups all-purpose flour
$2\frac{1}{2}$ teaspoons baking soda
$1\frac{1}{2}$ teaspoons ground ginger
$\frac{1}{2}$ teaspoon ground cinnamon
$\frac{1}{2}$ teaspoon ground mace
$\frac{1}{2}$ teaspoon ground cloves
$\frac{1}{2}$ teaspoon salt

$1\frac{1}{2}$ cups molasses
$\frac{1}{3}$ cup butter
$\frac{1}{3}$ cup solid vegetable shortening
$\frac{1}{2}$ cup firmly packed brown sugar
$\frac{1}{2}$ cup boiling water

Sift together the flour, baking soda, spices, and salt into a bowl. In another bowl, combine the molasses, butter, shortening, sugar, and boiling water. Beat on low speed with a mixer to break up the butter and shortening. Slowly add the dry ingredients and continue to mix until smooth. Cover the bowl and refrigerate until well chilled or overnight.

Preheat the oven to 375°F. Break the chilled dough into 4 equal pieces. On a well-floured surface, using a well-floured rolling pin, roll out each piece $\frac{1}{4}$-inch thick. Cut out the cookies with a floured $3\frac{1}{2}$-inch cookie cutter. Arrange the cookies on 2 ungreased baking sheets, spacing them well apart. Bake until slightly firm and cracked on top, about 12 minutes. Cool completely on a rack, then store in an airtight container. Makes about $2\frac{1}{2}$ dozen.

MEXICAN VANILLA BEAN ICE CREAM

6 egg yolks
1 cup sugar
$\frac{1}{8}$ teaspoon salt
2 cups milk
4 cups heavy cream
1 Mexican vanilla bean, or 2 tablespoons vanilla extract

Combine the egg yolks, sugar and salt in a heavy 3-quart saucepan and beat until pale and creamy. Meanwhile, in another pan, combine the milk and cream, split the vanilla bean in half lengthwise and, using the tip of a knife, scrape the seeds into the mixture. Heat over medium heat until the milk is scalded. Slowly add the hot milk to the yolk mixture, whisking constantly. Cook over moderately low heat, stirring constantly for several minutes, until the mixture is thick enough to coat the back of a spoon. Be careful not to heat the mixture too much or it will curdle. If it does curdle, add a few tablespoons of boiling water and beat like crazy. Add the vanilla extract, if using, and mix well. Remove from the heat and refrigerate until cold. Transfer to an ice-cream maker (in batches if necessary) and freeze according to the manufacturer's instructions. Makes about 2 quarts.

HEAVEN AND HELL CAKE
(continued from page 122)

For the **devil's food cake**, preheat the oven to 350°F. Sift the cocoa into a mixing bowl, then drizzle in the coffee, whisking to make a smooth paste. Set aside.

Combine the shortening, sugar, vanilla and eggs and beat for 2 minutes on medium speed.

In a separate bowl, sift together the flour, salt, baking powder and baking soda. Alternately add the cocoa-coffee mixture and the dry ingredients to the sugar-egg mixture and continue beating until incorporated. Pour the batter into an oiled and floured 10-inch cake pan and bake for 30 minutes.

To make the **peanut butter mousse**, in the bowl of an electric mixer whip the cream cheese until light and creamy. Gradually beat in the powdered sugar, then the peanut butter. Continue beating until thoroughly incorporated and fluffy.

Transfer the mixture to another bowl and set aside. Place the heavy cream in an electric mixer bowl and whip until stiff. Carefully but thoroughly, combine with the peanut butter mixture. Set aside.

In a saucepan, bring the cream for the ganache to a boil and stir in the chocolate. Cover the pan and let it melt. Whisk to combine thoroughly, then let cool to room temperature.

When both cakes have cooled, carefully slice them in half with a serrated knife so that you now have four layers. Place one layer of the devil's food cake on a cake plate and spoon one third of the peanut butter mousse on the top. Place a layer of the angel food on top of the mousse and spread with another one third of the peanut butter mousse. Continue layering until you have four layers of cake and three layers of mousse.

Whisk the ganache and spread with a spatula over the top and sides of the cake to frost generously. Chill in the refrigerator for at least 2 hours before serving. Serves 8 to 10.

Acknowledgments

Contributors

Scott Cohen may be a native of New York and a graduate of the Culinary Institute of America (CIA), but he has proven time and again that he is truly at home on the third coast. At Las Canarias since 1997, Cohen has moved beyond Tex-Mex and embraces the diverse culinary heritage of the Lone Star State to produce what he terms "comtemporary American regional [cuisine] with a French twist." He has worked in the nation's best hotel restaurants, including the Boca Raton Resort, the Stanhope Hotel in Manhattan, and Moulin des Mougins in the south of France.

Michael Cordua is a native of Nicaragua and a self-taught cook. In 1988 he opened Churrascos in Houston, featuring *churrasco* (a beef tenderloin basted with chimicurri), as well as many other dishes served up with pan-Latino flair. The success of Cordua's first restaurant led to the opening of two additional Houston-based venues, a second Churrascos, and Américas. Cordua has been named one of America's top ten chefs by *Food & Wine* and is the recipient of the Robert Mondavi Award for Culinary Excellence.

Nationally-acclaimed young chef **Danielle Custer** has come far in her career since graduating at the top of her class from the CIA in 1990. Recently named Best New Chef by *Food & Wine* magazine, Danielle has also made guest appearances at both the Aspen Food and Wine Classic and the James Beard House in New York. As executive chef and general manager of the five-star restaurant Laurels, Danielle takes her customers on a culinary adventure with her imaginative global cuisine and carefully crafted wine list.

In 1981, **Robert Del Grande** took a summer position in the kitchen of the newly opened Cafe Annie. The position grew into a long-term partnership, and his wife Mimi soon joined the restaurant as general manager. In 1992 Del Grande was the recipient of the James Beard Foundation's Best Chef Southwest award and, in 1997 and 1998, the restaurant was named one of America's Top Tables by *Gourmet Magazine*. The Del Grandes are currently pursuing other restaurant ventures, including Cafe Express, the Rio Ranch, and Taco Milagro.

Dotty Griffith is *The Dallas Morning News* Dining Editor and Restaurant Critic. A graduate of the University of Texas and Southern Methodist University, she's learned to eat well and enjoy life, and lives in Texas for the fabulous restaurants. In her own words: "The role of a critic is to let readers experience a restaurant through a review . . . to help them be smarter diners and consumers. More people eat than vote—I don't make dinner; I make reservations."

Classically trained at the CIA, **Dean Fearing** began his career at Maisonnette in Cincinnati, followed by The Pyramid Room at The Fairmont Hotel in Dallas. When The Mansion on Turtle Creek opened in 1980, Fearing came to the restaurant as executive sous chef, a position he resigned to become chef and part owner of the wildly successful Agnew's restaurant in Dallas. Shortly thereafter, Fearing returned to The Mansion on Turtle Creek in 1985, this time as position of executive chef, where he says he expects to remain "for at least twenty more years." He continues to develop Southwestern cuisine, using native wild game, chile peppers, and native herbs and vegetables.

Tim Keating began his culinary career in his early teens. Prior to joining The Four Seasons Hotel in Houston, Keating served as executive chef at the Omni Houston Hotel, and as sous chef at the Essex House in New York. Additionally, Keating worked as executive chef at the Ritz-Carlton in Houston. He honed his culinary talent at The Meridian Hotel in Newport Beach, California, where he teamed up with world-class chef Jacques Maximin. Chef Keating and his staff at the DeVille Restaurant have received *Gourmet* magazine's Reader's Choice award from 1997 through 1999, and six awards from the *Houston Zagat Restaurant Survey* in 1999.

Chefs **Bruce and Susan Molzan** met each other while attending James Madison University in Virginia. Bruce went on to the Culinary Institute of America where he graduated at the top of his class, and in 1986 they purchased the Ruggles Grill in Houston. Susan pursued her interest in pastries, which has earned her national recognition. The Ruggles Grill has received the Ivy Award and a Zagat award. With four restaurants and another opening at Enron Field in the spring of 2000, the Molzans have achieved fabulous culinary success.

Monica Pope is executive chef and owner of the Boulevard Bistrot, a neighborhood restaurant serving eclectic American food in Houston's Museum District. In the year 2000, Monica's more casual, counter-style restaurant, 43 Brasserie, opens just two doors from Boulevard Bistrot, providing a wonderful synergy to the neighborhood. Monica is best known for her unexpected combinations of ingredients and daring presentations of bold and subtle flavors. Monica is a charter member of the Chefs Collaborative 2000, and champions sustainability in local agriculture, product purchasing, and restaurant recycling.

Stephan Pyles is acknowledged as one of the founding fathers of Southwestern cuisine and was the first Texan inducted into *Who's Who of Food and Wine in America*. His Dallas-based Star Canyon was named one of the top five new restaurants in America by the James Beard Foundation and, most recently, it was named the restaurant that "Best Reflects Dallas" in the July 1999 issue of *Food & Wine*. His water-themed restaurant, Aqua-Knox, opened in Dallas in November 1997, features sophisticated global cuisine. In May 1999, Pyles opened Star Canyon and Taqueria Cañonita in Las Vegas at The Venetian; and in November 1999, he premiered Fishbowl—a "sixties pan-Asian" destination—located adjacent to AquaKnox.

Grady Spears worked as a cowhand and cattle broker before becoming executive chef and co-owner of the Reata Restaurants in Alpine and Fort Worth, Texas and in Beverly Hills. His work at Reata has also been widely praised in newspapers and magazines coast to coast, including the *New York Times*, *Texas Monthly*, and *Martha Stuart Living*. He is the author of *A Cowboy in the Kitchen* and *Cowboy Cocktails*. Grady divides his time between Alpine, Fort Worth, and Beverly Hills, but anywhere in Texas is truly home!

Michael Velardi, executive chef at Pappas Brothers Steakhouse in Houston, puts his culinary emphasis on elegant simplicity. His patrons are never misled, however, for his tenure at the Steakhouse bespeaks a vast experience and a diverse team of chefs. Before joining Pappas Brothers, Velardi worked as chef at Gordon's and Jovan's in Chicago, and at the Bel Air Hotel and L'Ermitage in Los Angeles. In Houston, he worked for both The Grotto and La Griglia restaurants. Since opening in 1995, Pappas Brother's Steakhouse has earned *Texas Monthly*'s Best Big-City Steakhouse, *Wine Spectator*'s Best of Excellence Award, and *Zagat*'s America's Top Restaurants award.

Sources

Pages 34-37: Nambe Platter from Stanley Korshak

Pages 40-41: Dishes, rack, and napkin from Stanley Korshak

Pages 42-43: Bowl and tray from Pottery Barn

Pages 44-45: Rainbow bowl from Saks 5th Avenue, Houston

Pages 46-47: Platter from Modern Art Museum of Fort Worth; cutlery and napkin from Stanley Korshak; napkin holder, charger, and table decoration from Jan Barbolglio

Pages 48-49: Soup bowl from Stanley Korshak; platter and spoon from Lady Primrose

Pages 50-51: Dish and napkin from Stanley Korshak; chargers from Jan Barboglio

Pages 52-53: Place mat from Stanley Korshak; serving tray from Jan Barboglio

Pages 54-55: Bowl, salad service, and candle holder from Lady Primrose, Dallas

Pages 56-57: Plate, napkin and tray from Stanley Korshak

Pages 58-59: Fork from Stanley Korshak; charger, pie dish and serving tray from Jan Barboglio

Pages 66-67: Dish from Crate & Barrel; cutlery from Pottery Barn; placemat from Saks 5th Avenue

Pages 68-69: Table setting from Essential Settings

Pages 70-71: Plate from Pottery Barn

Pages 72-73: Dish and charger from Jan Barboglio; cutlery and napkin from Stanley Korshak

Pages 74-75: Charger from Pottery Barn

Pages 76-77: Plate and charger from Pottery Barn

Pages 80-81: Schnapps glass from Crate & Barrel

Pages 82-83: Plate and glass from Pottery Barn; three-part dish from Crate & Barrel

Pages 84-85: Table setting from Village Weavers; brass plate and tray courtesy of Todd Roesler

Pages 84-85: Plate and cutlery from River Square Antiques

Pages 86-87: Plate and Glass from Pottery Barn; cutlery from Crate & Barrel

Pages 92-93: Plate, cutlery, and wine glass from Essential Settings

Pages 94-95: Plate and cutlery from Pottery Barn

Pages 96-97: Platter, salt & pepper shaker, and fruit bowl from Essential Settings

Pages 104-105: Iron platters and containers by Jan Barboglio

Pages 106-107: Plate from Events, Houston

Pages 108-109: Beaded mat from Stanley Korshak; charger from Jan Barbolglio

Pages 110-111: Tray from the Modern Art Museum of Fort Worth

Pages 112-113: Plate and cutlery from River Square Antiques; table setting from Village Weavers

Pages 114-115: Plate from Pier 1; art from Realto

Pages 116-117: Napkins and tray from Stanley Korshak

Pages 118-119: Plate from Crate & Barrel; vase from Saks 5th Avenue

Pages 120-121: Cloth, party hat, and fringe collar from Village Weavers

Pages 122-123: platter and stand from Pottery Barn

Shops and Artists

Jan Barboglio, 145 Cole, Dallas, Texas 75207. Tel: 214/698-1920; Fax: 214/698-8611

Crate & Barrel
A home furnishing retailer specializing in tabletop, kitchenware and giftware. In some of its 80 stores, the accessories collection is joined by a complete and eclectic furniture selection. For information on the store nearest you, call 1-800-996-9960

Essential Settings, 1716 Post Oak Boulevard, Houston, Texas 77056. Tel: 713/629-6244; Fax: 713/629-5677

Events, River Oaks Shopping Center, 1966 West Gray, Houston 77019. Tel: 713/520-5700; Fax: 713/528-2301

Lacquer Images, specializing in lacquer overlay of Print Art, Photographs, Documents, and Certificates. 381 West 7th Street, San Pedro, California, 90731 Tel/Fax: 310/514-9300

Lady Primrose's Shopping English Countryside is a grand store in a fantasy setting, offering unusual antique furniture, decorative accessories, and new gift items. In addition, the store has emerged as a popular and innovative resource for design ideas and applications. The Crescent, 500 Crescent Court, Suite 154, Dallas, Texas 75201. Tel: 800/525-5066; Fax: 214/871-8339

Modern Art Museum of Fort Worth
1309 Montgomery Street at Camp Bowie Boulevard, Fort Worth, Texas, 76107. Tel: 871/738-9215; Fax: 817/735-1161

Pier 1 Imports
510 Houston, Fort Worth, Texas 76102. Tel: 817/877-0479

Pottery Barn
One of the nations leading specialty retailers of home furnishings and decorative accessories, Pottery Barn now features a "design studio" where customers can sketch out a floorplan of their living space and then coordinate floor coverings, fabrics, furniture, and window treatments. To receive a catalog, place an order, or find the store nearest you, please call 800-922-9934

River Square Antiques
Collectibles, and Gifts, 514 River Walk San Antonio, Texas 78205. Tel: 210/224-0900

Stanley Korshak
Located amid the beautiful architecture of the Crescent, Stanley Korshak is a Dallas landmark. This specialty store offers unique designer merchandise including a home collection, a linen boutique, fine apparel for men and women and precious jewelry. 500 Crescent Court, Suite 100, Dallas, Texas 75201. Tel: 214/871-3600 www.stanleykorshak.com

Village Weavers
Located in historic La Villita, San Antonio, and features unique handwoven clothing, accessories, hats, rugs, wallhangings, baskets, pottery and jewelry. The very friendly staff will assist you in finding special gifts for personal and home use. Tel: 210/222-0776. 418 Villita, San Antonio, Texas 78205. www.villageweavers.com

The publisher would especially like to thank Ken Lovering, Shelly Rutledge, Phil Bentley, and J.U. Salvant.

We are particularly grateful to the restaurant and executive staff members who made this book possible, including:

Reata Restaurant
Reggie Ferguson
Todd Phillips, *Executive Sous Chef*
Tim Love, *Executive Sous Chef*
Sarah Spears, *Private Dining Coordinator*
Mary Margaret Spikes, *Assistant*

Star Canyon
Matthew Dunn, *Executive Chef*
Sharon Kagan, *Executive Assistant*

Laurels
Mark Crowder, *Sous Chef*

Café Annie
Ben Berryhill
Elliott Kelly, *Sous Chef*
Randall Knight
Tyla Miller, *Assistant and Manager*

The Mansion on Turtle Creek
Ashley Young, *Marketing Coordinator*
Patricia Sullivan, *Director of Marketing*
Shannon Swindle, *Pastry Chef*

Beth Huch, *Culinary Administrator*

Américas
Luis Sanchez, *Corporate Chef*
Tom Lower, *Manager*
Gumaro Lopez, *Executive Chef*
Bill Floyd
Holly Wall, *Assistant*

DeVille Restaurant
Vanessa Molina, *Assistant*

Ruggles Grill
Andreas Becker, *Corporate Chef*
Courtney Gasow, *Assistant*
Susan Molzan, *Pastry Chef*
Gilbert Buyher, *Chef de Cuisine*

Boulevard Bistrot
Andrea Butler, *Executive Assistant*

Las Canarias
Eric Nelson, *Chef de Cuisine*
Jane Satel, *PR Director*
Todd Roesler, *Executive Assistant Manager*
Beth Ticku, *Sales and Marketing*

Pappas Bros. Steakhouse
Brent Trudeau, *Corporate Chef*
Tim Kohler, *Manager*

Hunter Brother's Ranch
Jeff Vara, *Operations Manager*
Paul Bentley, *Bartender*
Brad Cromar, *Manager*

Recipe testing and Caroline Stuart's food for photography prepared by **Allen Smith** and **Glenn Wilkes**.

Index